# SECRET CODES 2004

## VOLUME 1

PlayStation® 2 . . . . . . . . . . . . . . . . . . . . . . . .2

PlayStation® . . . . . . . . . . . . . . . . . . . . . . . . .83

Xbox™ . . . . . . . . . . . . . . . . . . . . . . . . . . . .106

GameCube™ . . . . . . . . . . . . . . . . . . . . . .176

Game Boy® Advance . . . . . . . . . . . . . . .228

**||||||BRADYGAMES®**
TAKE YOUR GAME FURTHER®

# Games List

AMPLITUDE . . . . . . . . . . . . . . . . . . . . . . . . . . . . . . .5

ATV OFFROAD FURY 2 . . . . . . . . . . . . . . . . . . . . . . .6

BATMAN: RISE OF SIN TZU . . . . . . . . . . . . . . . . . . .8

BATTLE ENGINE AQUILA . . . . . . . . . . . . . . . . . . . .8

BIG MUTHA TRUCKERS . . . . . . . . . . . . . . . . . . . .9

CASTLEVANIA: LAMENT OF INNOCENCE . . . . . . . .9

DEAD TO RIGHTS . . . . . . . . . . . . . . . . . . . . . . . . . .11

DEF JAM VENDETTA . . . . . . . . . . . . . . . . . . . . . . .13

DEVIL MAY CRY 2 . . . . . . . . . . . . . . . . . . . . . . . . .17

DOWNHILL DOMINATION . . . . . . . . . . . . . . . . . .17

DR. MUTO . . . . . . . . . . . . . . . . . . . . . . . . . . . . . . .18

ENTER THE MATRIX . . . . . . . . . . . . . . . . . . . . . . .19

EVOLUTION SKATEBOARDING . . . . . . . . . . . . . .19

FINDING NEMO . . . . . . . . . . . . . . . . . . . . . . . . . .19

FREEDOM FIGHTERS . . . . . . . . . . . . . . . . . . . . . .21

FREESTYLE METAL X . . . . . . . . . . . . . . . . . . . . . . .22

FUTURAMA . . . . . . . . . . . . . . . . . . . . . . . . . . . . . .23

GRAND THEFT AUTO: VICE CITY . . . . . . . . . . . . .25

HIGH HEAT MAJOR LEAGUE BASEBALL 2004 . . . . .30

HITMAN 2: SILENT ASSASSIN . . . . . . . . . . . . . . . .30

HULK . . . . . . . . . . . . . . . . . . . . . . . . . . . . . . . . . . .31

HUNTER: THE RECKONING WAYWARD . . . . . . . .32

JAMES BOND 007: NIGHTFIRE . . . . . . . . . . . . . . .33

JURASSIC PARK: OPERATION GENESIS . . . . . . . . .37

MIDNIGHT CLUB II . . . . . . . . . . . . . . . . . . . . . . . .39

MINORITY REPORT . . . . . . . . . . . . . . . . . . . . . . .40

MLB 2004 . . . . . . . . . . . . . . . . . . . . . . . . . . . . . . .42

## PlayStation® 2

MLB SLUGFEST 20-04 . . . . . . . . . . . . . . . . . . . . . .43

NASCAR: DIRT TO DAYTONA . . . . . . . . . . . . . . . . . .46

NASCAR THUNDER . . . . . . . . . . . . . . . . . . . . . . .46

NBA 2K3 . . . . . . . . . . . . . . . . . . . . . . . . . . . . . . .47

NBA LIVE 2003 . . . . . . . . . . . . . . . . . . . . . . . . . . .47

NBA STREET VOL. 2 . . . . . . . . . . . . . . . . . . . . . . .49

PRIMAL . . . . . . . . . . . . . . . . . . . . . . . . . . . . . . . .51

PRO RACE DRIVER . . . . . . . . . . . . . . . . . . . . . . . .52

RATCHET AND CLANK . . . . . . . . . . . . . . . . . . . . . .52

ROCKY . . . . . . . . . . . . . . . . . . . . . . . . . . . . . . . .53

RTX RED ROCK . . . . . . . . . . . . . . . . . . . . . . . . . .54

RUN LIKE HELL . . . . . . . . . . . . . . . . . . . . . . . . . .55

SHOX . . . . . . . . . . . . . . . . . . . . . . . . . . . . . . . . .56

SILENT HILL 3 . . . . . . . . . . . . . . . . . . . . . . . . . . .57

SIMPSONS SKATEBOARDING . . . . . . . . . . . . . . . . .59

SOCCER SLAM . . . . . . . . . . . . . . . . . . . . . . . . . . .60

SPEED KINGS . . . . . . . . . . . . . . . . . . . . . . . . . . .62

STARSKY AND HUTCH . . . . . . . . . . . . . . . . . . . . . .64

SUMMER HEAT BEACH VOLLEYBALL . . . . . . . . . . . .64

TENCHU: WRATH OF HEAVEN . . . . . . . . . . . . . . . . .67

THE GETAWAY . . . . . . . . . . . . . . . . . . . . . . . . . . .68

THE GREAT ESCAPE . . . . . . . . . . . . . . . . . . . . . . .69

THE LORD OF THE RINGS: THE TWO TOWERS . . . .70

THE SIMPSONS: HIT & RUN . . . . . . . . . . . . . . . . . .71

THE SIMS . . . . . . . . . . . . . . . . . . . . . . . . . . . . . .73

TIGER WOODS PGA TOUR 2004 . . . . . . . . . . . . . . .74

TOM AND JERRY: WAR OF THE WHISKERS . . . . . . .76

TOMB RAIDER: THE ANGEL OF DARKNESS . . . . . . .76

TONY HAWK'S PRO SKATER 4 . . . . . . . . . . . . . . . . .77

WAKEBOARDING UNLEASHED . . . . . . . . . . . . . . . .79

WHIRL TOUR . . . . . . . . . . . . . . . . . . . . . . . . . . . . . .80

WHITEOUT . . . . . . . . . . . . . . . . . . . . . . . . . . . . . . . .80

X2 WOLVERINE'S REVENGE . . . . . . . . . . . . . . . . . . .81

YU-GI-OH! THE DUELIST OF THE ROSES . . . . . . . .81

ZONE OF THE ENDERS: THE 2ND RUNNER . . . . . .82

# AMPLITUDE

**Blur**

During a game, press R3 (x4), L3 (x4), R3.

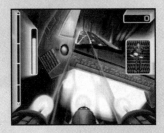

**Monkey Notes**

During a game, press L3 (x4), R3 (x4), L3. Quit the game and go back into the song to see the effect. Reenter to disable.

**Random Note Placement**

During a game, press **X**, **X**, Left, Left, R3, R3, Right, Right. Quit the game and go back into the song to see the effect. Reenter to disable.

**Change Shape of Track Layout**

During the game, press L3 (x3), R3 (x3), L3, R3, L3. Quit the game and go back into the song to see the effect. Enter it once for a tunnel look and a second time for a Tempest-style look. Enter a third time to disable.

# ATV OFFROAD FURY 2

Select Profile Editor, Unlock Items, then Cheats, and enter the following:

**Unlock Everything**
Enter **IGIVEUP**.

**All ATVs**
Enter **SHOWROOM**.

**All Equipment**
Enter **THREADS**.

**All Tracks**
Enter **TRLBLAZR**.

**San Jacinto Isles**

Enter **GABRIEL**.

**All Games**

Enter **GAMEON**.

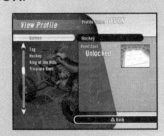

**All Championship Events**

Enter **GOLDCUPS**.

**1,000 Profile Points**

Enter **GIMMEPTS**.

### Disable Wrecks

Enter **FLYPAPER**. Reenter the code to enable wrecks again.

### Aggressive AI

Enter **EATDIRT**. Reenter the code to disable aggressive AI.

# BATMAN: RISE OF SIN TZU

### Unlimited Health

Pause the game, hold L1 + L2 + R1 + R2 and press Up, Right, Down, Left, Up, Left, Down, Right.

### All Upgrades

Pause the game, hold L1 + L2 + R1 + R2 and press Up, Up, Left, Left, Right, Right, Down, Down.

### End Game Rewards

Pause the game, hold L1 + L2 + R1 + R2 and press Down, Up, Down, Up, Left, Right, Left, Right.

### Unlimited Combo Meter

Pause the game, hold L1 + L2 + R1 + R2 and press Left, Right, Up, Down, Right, Left, Down, Up.

### Dark Knight Difficulty

Pause the game, hold L1 + L2 + R1 + R2 and press Down, Left, Right, Up, Up, Right, Left, Down.

# BATTLE ENGINE AQUILA

### Level Select

Start a new game and enter **!EVAH!** as a name.

### God Mode

Start a new game and enter **B4K42** as a name. Pause the game to find this option.

### All Extras

Start a new game and enter **105770Y2** as a name.

# BIG MUTHA TRUCKERS

**All Cheats**

Enter CHEATINGMUTHATRUCKER as a code.

**Evil Truck**

Enter VARLEY as a code.

**Fast Truck**

Enter GINGERBEER as a code.

**$10 Million**

Enter LOTSAMONEY as a code.

**Level Select**

Enter LAZYPLAYER as a code.

**Unlimited Time**

Enter PUBLICTRANSPORT as a code.

**Disable Damage**

Enter 6WL as a code.

**Automatic Sat Nav**

Enter USETHEFORCE as a code.

**Diplomatic Immunity**

Enter VICTORS as a code.

**Small Pedestrians**

Enter DAISHI as a code.

**Bonus Levels**

Enter JINGLEBELLS as a code in the options screen.

# CASTLEVANIA: LAMENT OF INNOCENCE

**Joachim Mode**

After clearing the game with Leon once, enter **@JOACHIM** into the name entry screen to access this mode. This allows you to play through the game as the character Joachim. You do not use sub-weapons, any items, or equipment in this mode. Instead, you have new commands to use.

| Left analog stick | Move your character |
|---|---|
| R1/R2 button | Lock onto nearest enemy |
| Left analog + R1 | Move while locking onto and facing nearest enemy. If no enemy is nearby, move while facing in one direction. |
| Left analog + R1 + **X** | Dash |
| ■ | Sword throw attack. If you hold the button down before releasing it, the attack grows in strength |
| ▲ | Toggle between Joachim's two stances |
| ● | Consume MP to use a special attack. (MP is regained through damaging enemies) |
| **X** | Jump. Press twice to double-jump |

## Crazy Mode

This Mode is also opened after defeating the game once with Leon. Enter **@CRAZY** into the name entry screen to play through in this difficult game mode. You play as Leon, but the difficulty is greatly increased. More monsters appear to swarm you, and less damage is performed with each attack.

## Skills Mode

Although it is not listed after defeating the game, this mode is unlocked after you clear the game with Leon. Enter **@LLSKILL** into the name screen to begin a normal new game with all of the weapon skills.

## Pumpkin Mode

Once you've managed to defeat the game in Joachim Mode, a new Mode opens: Pumpkin Mode. Enter **@PUMPKIN** as your name to play through as this new character. The new Pumpkin sub-weapon is used in this mode.

## Boss Rush

After you've cleared the game with Leon and defeated
all of the Bosses, you can return to your save game and
attempt to defeat the Boss Rush. To access this, enter
the platform room. A new glowing circle of light is now
in the center of the platforms. Step onto this circle to
enter the Boss Rush. In this mode, you fight the various
Bosses of the game in a row. After each one you have a
chance to recover a few Hearts and Potions.

# DEAD TO RIGHTS

From the Main Menu, hold L1 + L2 + R1 + R2 and enter
the following cheats:

## Lazy Mode

Down, Left, Down, ▲, Down

## 10,000 Bullets Mode

Up, Left, Down, Right, ●

## Time To Play

■, ■, ●, ●, Right

**One Shot Kill**
▲, ●, ●, ●, Left

**Sharpshooter Mode**
■, ■, ■, Down, Right

**Bang-bang Cheat**
●, ▲, ■, ●, Right

**Precursor**
Up, Up, Down, Down, Up

**Super Cop Mode**
■, ▲, Left, Up, Right

**Woof!**
●, ■, ▲, ●, Down. This gives Shadow infinite stamina.

**Gimme Some Sugar, Baby**
Left, Right, Left, ●, ■. This gives infinite adrenaline.

**Bulletproof Mode**
Up, Up, Up, ■, Down

**Chow Yun Jack Mode**
▲, ●, Up, Up, Up

**Up Close and Personal Mode**
■, ▲, ●, ▲, ■

**Your Skills are Extraordinary**
●, ●, Up, Up, ■

**Fight Club**
Right, ■, Left, ●, ▲

**Jack Off**
▲, ▲, Up, Up, ▲

**Boomstick Mode**
Right, ●, ●, ●, ■

**Hard Boiled Mode**
▲, ■, Left, Left, ●

**Wussy Mode**
■, Left, ▲, Up, Down

# DEF JAM VENDETTA

## Arii

At the character select, hold L1 + L2 + R1 + R2 and press **X**, **■**, **▲**, **●**, **■**.

## Briggs Alternate Costume

At the character select, hold L1 + L2 + R1 + R2 and press **X**, **▲**, **●**, **■**, **●**.

## Carla

At the character select, hold L1 + L2 + R1 + R2 and press **X**, **■**, X (x3).

## Chukklez

At the character select, hold L1 + L2 + R1 + R2 and press **■**, **■**, **▲**, **X**, **●**.

## Cruz

At the character select, hold L1 + L2 + R1 + R2 and press **●**, **▲**, **X**, **X**, **●**.

## D-Mob

At the character select, hold L1 + L2 + R1 + R2 and press **■**, **■**, **▲**, **■**, **■**.

## Dan G

At the character select, hold L1 + L2 + R1 + R2 and press **X**, **●**, **X**, **●**, **■**.

## Deebo

At the character select, hold L1 + L2 + R1 + R2 and press **●**, **●**, **X**, **X**, **▲**.

## Deja

At the character select, hold L1 + L2 + R1 + R2 and press **●**, **■**, **●**, **●**, **X**.

## DMX

At the character select, hold L1 + L2 + R1 + R2 and press **●**, **X**, **●**, **▲**, **■**.

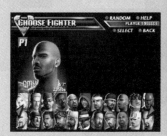

## Drake: Alternate Costume

**X**, **▲**, **▲**, **●**, **●**

### Funkmaster Flex

At the character select, hold L1 + L2 + R1 + R2 and press ●, ▲, ●, ●, ■.

### Headache

At the character select, hold L1 + L2 + R1 + R2 and press ▲(x3), ■, ●.

### House

At the character select, hold L1 + L2 + R1 + R2 and press ▲, X, ▲, ●, X.

### Iceberg

At the character select, hold L1 + L2 + R1 + R2 and press ■, ▲, ●, ■, ●.

### Ludacris

At the character select, hold L1 + L2 + R1 + R2 and press ●(3), ■, ▲.

### Manny Alternate Costume

At the character select, hold L1 + L2 + R1 + R2 and press ●, ■, ●, ■, ●.

### Masa

At the character select, hold L1 + L2 + R1 + R2 and press X, ●, ▲, ■, ■.

### Method Man

At the character select, hold L1 + L2 + R1 + R2 and press ■, ●, X, ▲, ●.

### Moses

At the character select, hold L1 + L2 + R1 + R2 and press ▲, ▲, ■, ■, X.

### N.O.R.E.

At the character select, hold L1 + L2 + R1 + R2 and press ●, ■, ▲, X, ●.

### Nyne

At the character select, hold L1 + L2 + R1 + R2 and press ■, ●, X, X, ▲.

### Omar

At the character select, hold L1 + L2 + R1 + R2 and press ●, ●, ■, ▲, ▲.

### Opal

At the character select, hold L1 + L2 + R1 + R2 and press ●, ●, ■, ■, ▲.

## Peewee

At the character select, hold L1 + L2 + R1 + R2 and press X, X, ■, ▲, ■.

## Peewee Alternate Costume

At the character select, hold L1 + L2 + R1 + R2 and press X, ▲, ▲, ■, ●.

## Penny

At the character select, hold L1 + L2 + R1 + R2 and press X (x3), ▲, ●.

## Pockets

At the character select, hold L1 + L2 + R1 + R2 and press ▲, ■, ●, ■, X.

## Proof Alternate Costume

At the character select, hold L1 + L2 + R1 + R2 and press X, ■, ▲, ■, ●.

## Razor

At the character select, hold L1 + L2 + R1 + R2 and press ▲, ■, ▲, ●, X.

## Razor Alternate Costume

At the character select, hold L1 + L2 + R1 + R2 and press ■, ●, X, ▲, ▲.

## Redman

At the character select, hold L1 + L2 + R1 + R2 and press ●, ●, ▲, ■, X.

## Ruffneck

At the character select, hold L1 + L2 + R1 + R2 and press X, ■, X, ▲, ●.

## Ruffneck Alternate Costume

At the character select, hold L1 + L2 + R1 + R2 and press ■, ●, ▲, X, ■.

## Scarface

At the character select, hold L1 + L2 + R1 + R2 and press ●, ■, X, ▲, ■.

## Sketch

At the character select, hold L1 + L2 + R1 + R2 and press ▲, ▲, ●, ■, X.

### Snowman

At the character select, hold L1 + L2 + R1 + R2 and press ▲, ▲, X, X, ●.

### Spider Alternate Costume

At the character select, hold L1 + L2 + R1 + R2 and press ■, ▲, X, ■, ●.

### Steel

At the character select, hold L1 + L2 + R1 + R2 and press X, ▲, ●, ●, ▲.

### Tank Alternate Costume

At the character select, hold L1 + L2 + R1 + R2 and press ▲, ■, ●, X, X.

### T'ai

At the character select, hold L1 + L2 + R1 + R2 and press ●, ●, ■, X, ●.

### Zaheer

At the character select, hold L1 + L2 + R1 + R2 and press ▲, ▲, ■, X, X.

# DEVIL MAY CRY 2

**Dante and Lucia Bonus Diesel Costume**

Play the first mission and save. Reset the game and at the Press Start screen, press L3, R3, L1, R1, L2, R2, L3, R3.

# DOWNHILL DOMINATION

During a game, press Up, ▲, Down, **X**, Left, ●, Right, ■. Then enter the following:

**More Cash**

Right, Up, Up, ●, ●, ■

**Energy Restore**

Down, Right, Right, Left, Left

**Adrenaline Boost**

Down, Left, Left, Right

**Stoke Trick Meter**

Down, Left, Left, Right, Right

**Super Bunny Hop**

Up, **X**, Left, ■, Up

**Super Bounce**

Left, ■, **X**, Up, ▲

**Mega Flip**

Right, Up, Up, Right, Right, ■

**Anti Gravity**

Down, ▲, ■, ■, Up

**Combat Upgrade**

Up, Down, Left, Left, Right

**Upgrade to Bottle**

Up, Down, Left, Left, Right, Right

**Combat Free**

Left, ■, ●, ■, Left

# DR. MUTO

Select Cheats from the Options and enter the following:

**Invincibility**

Enter **NECROSCI**. This doesn't help you when you fall from high above.

**Never Take Damage**

Enter **CHEATERBOY**.

**Unlock Every Gadget**

Enter **TINKERTOY**.

**Unlock Every Morph**

Enter **EUREKA**.

**Go Anywhere**

Enter **BEAMMEUP**.

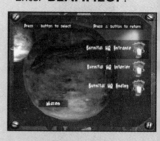

**Secret Morphs**

Enter **LOGGLOGG**.

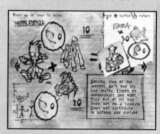

**See The Movies**

Enter **HOTTICKET**.

**Super Ending**

Enter **BUZZOFF**.

# ENTER THE MATRIX

### Cheats

After playing through the hacking system and unlocking
CHEAT.EXE, you can use CHEAT.EXE to enter the following:

| | |
|---|---|
| Infinite Ammo | 1DDF2556 |
| All Guns | 0034AFFF |
| Invisibility | FFFFFFF1 |
| Infinite Focus | 69E5D9E4 |
| Infinite Health | 7F4DF451 |
| Speedy Logos | 7867F443 |
| Unlock Secret Level | 13D2C77F |

# EVOLUTION SKATEBOARDING

### All Secret Characters

Press Up, Down, Left, Right, Up, Down, Left, Right, Up,
Down, Left, Right, ●.

### Level Select

Press L2, R2, Left, Right, Left, Right, Left, Right, Down,
Down, Up, Up, Down, Up.

# FINDING NEMO

Enter the following at the main menu. The word Cheat! will
appear if entered correctly. Pause the game at the level
select to access the cheats.

## Level Select

Press ▲, ▲, ▲, ■, ■, ●, ■, ▲, ●, ■, ▲, ■, ▲, ■, ▲, ●, ▲, ▲.

## Invincibility

Press ▲, ■, ■, ●, ●, ●, ▲, ▲, ■, ■, ■, ● (x4), ■, ▲, ●, ●, ●, ■, ●, ▲, ●, ●, ■, ●, ●, ▲, ●, ■, ●, ●, ●, ▲.

## Credits

Press ▲, ■, ●, ▲, ▲, ■, ●, ▲, ■, ●, ▲, ■, ■, ●, ▲, ■, ●, ▲, ■, ●, ●, ▲, ■, ●.

## Secret Level

Press ▲, ■, ●, ●, ■, ▲, ▲, ■, ●, ●, ■, ▲, ▲, ●, ■, ▲, ■, ●, ●, ■, ▲.

# FREEDOM FIGHTERS

**Cheat List**

During the game, enter the following:

| | |
|---|---|
| Invisibility | ▲, X, ■, ●, ●, Left |
| Infinite ammo | ▲, X, ■, ●, X, Right |
| Max charisma | ▲, X, ■, ●, X Down |
| Heavy machine gun | ▲, X, ■, ●, ▲, Down |
| Nail gun | ▲, X, ■, ●, X, Left |
| Rocket launcher | ▲, X, ■, ●, ▲, Left |
| Shotgun | ▲, X, ■, ●, ●, Up |
| Sniper rifle | ▲, X, ■, ●, ▲, Right |
| Sub machine gun | ▲, X, ■, ●, ▲, Up |
| Ragdolls | ▲, X, ■, ●, ■, Up |
| Slow motion | ▲, X, ■, ●, ●, Right |
| Fast motion | ▲, X, ■, ●, ●, Down |
| Change spawn point | ▲, X, ■, ●, X, Up |

# FREESTYLE METAL X

Select Cheats from the Options and enter the following:

**All Riders And Bikes**
Enter dudemaster.

**All Outfits**
Enter johnnye.

**All Bike Parts**
Enter garageking.

**$1,000,000**
Enter sugardaddy.

**All The Special Stunt Slots**
Enter fleximan.

### All Rider, Babe and Making of Posters

Enter seeall.

### All Songs

Enter hearall.

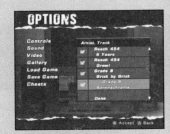

### All Videos

Enter watchall.

# FUTURAMA

While playing, hold L1 + L2 until the screen flashes. Then enter the following:

### Full Health

Enter Down, ■, ▲, Down, ■, ▲, ●, X, R2, Up, Select

### Invincibility

Down, ■, ▲, Down, ■, ▲, ●, X, R2, ▲, Select

### Unlock All Extras

Down, ■, ▲, Down, ■, ▲, ●, X, R2, ●, Select

### Full Charge

Down, ■, ▲, Down, ■, ▲, ●, X, R2, Left, Select

### Extra Five Lives

Down, ■, ▲, Down, ■, ▲, ●, X, R2, Down, Select

## Unlimited Ammunition

Down, ■, ▲, Down, ■, ▲, ●, X, R2, Right, Select

## Level Select

While playing, hold L1 + L2 until the screen flashes. Then enter the following:

| Level | Code |
|---|---|
| Planet Express | Down, ■, ▲, Down, ■, ▲, ■, ▲, Up, Up, Select |
| Sewers | Down, ■, ▲, Down, ■, ▲, ■, ▲, Up, Right, Select |
| Subway | Down, ■, ▲, Down, ■, ▲, ■, ▲, Up, Down, Select |
| Old New York | Down, ■, ▲, Down, ■, ▲, ■, ▲, Up, Left, Select |
| Red Light District | Down, ■, ▲, Down, ■, ▲, ■, ▲, Up, ▲, Select |
| Uptown | Down, ■, ▲, Down, ■, ▲, ■, ▲, Up, ●, Select |
| New New York | Down, ■, ▲, Down, ■, ▲, ■, ▲, Up, X, Select |
| Canyon | Down, ■, ▲, Down, ■, ▲, ■, ▲, Right, Up, Select |
| Mine | Down, ■, ▲, Down, ■, ▲, ■, ▲, Right, Right, Select |
| Mine Tunnel | Down, ■, ▲, Down, ■, ▲, ■, ▲, Right, Down, Select |
| Junkyard 1 | Down, ■, ▲, Down, ■, ▲, ■, ▲, Right, Left, Select |
| Junkyard 2 | Down, ■, ▲, Down, ■, ▲, ■, ▲, Right, ▲, Select |
| Juunkyard 3 | Down, ■, ▲, Down, ■, ▲, ■, ▲, Right, ●, Select |
| Market Square | Down, ■, ▲, Down, ■, ▲, ■, ▲, Down, Up, Select |
| Left Wing | Down, ■, ▲, Down, ■, ▲, ■, ▲, Down, Right, Select |
| Right Wing | Down, ■, ▲, Down, ■, ▲, ■, ▲, Down, Down, Select |
| Temple Courtyard | Down, ■, ▲, Down, ■, ▲, ■, ▲, Down, Left, Select |
| Inner Temple | Down, ■, ▲, Down, ■, ▲, ■, ▲, Down, ▲, Select |

| Bogad's Swamp | Down, ■, ▲, Down, ■, ▲, ■, ▲, Left, Up, Select |
| Mom's HQ – Bender | Down, ■, ▲, Down, ■, ▲, ■, ▲, ▲, Up, Select |
| Mom's HQ – Leela | Down, ■, ▲, Down, ■, ▲, ■, ▲, ▲, Right, Select |
| Mom's HQ – Fry | Down, ■, ▲, Down, ■, ▲, ■, ▲, ▲, Down, Select |

# GRAND THEFT AUTO: VICE CITY

Enter the following cheats during a game. Some of these cheats may affect your game play. Don't save your progress, unless you are sure you want this effect.

**Health Cheat**
R1, R2, L1, CR, Left, Down, Right, Up, Left, Down, Right, Up

**Armor Cheat**
R1, R2, L1, X, Left, Down, Right, Up, Left, Down, Right, Up

**Low Gravity**
Right, R2, CR, R1, L2, Down, L1, R1

**Better Driving**
▲, R1, R1, Left, R1, L1, R2, L1 Use L3 to jump vehicle.

**Suicide**
Right, L2, Down, R1, Left, Left, R1, L1, L2, L1

**Wanted Level Up 2**
R1, R1, ●, R2, Left, Right, Left, Right, Left, Right

**Wanted Level Down 2**
R1, R1, ●, R2, Up, Down, Up, Down, Up, Down

**Slow Motion**
▲, Up, Right, Down, ■, R2, R1

**Faster Time**
●, ●, L1, ■, L1, ■, ■, ■, L1, ▲, ●, ▲

**Black Cars**
●, L2, Up, R1, Left, X, R1, L1, Left, ●

**Pink Cars**
●, L1, Down, L2, Left, X, R1, L1, Right, ●

25

**Change Wheels**
R1, **X**, **▲**, Right, R2, **■**, Up, Down, **■**

**Cars Float**
Right, R2, **●**, R1, L2, **■**, R1, R2

**All Cars Explode**
R2, L2, R1, L1, L2, R2, **■**, **▲**, **●**, **▲**, L2, L1

**Robocops**
**●**, L1, Down, L2, Left, **X**, R1, L1, Right, **X**

**Cars Don't Stop**
R2, **●**, R1, L2, Left, R1, L1, R2, L2

**Pedestrians Riot**
Down, Left, Up, Left, **X**, R2, R1, L2, L1

**Pedestrians Attack**
Down, Up, Up, Up, **X**, R2, R1, L2, L2

**Pedestrians Have Weapon**
R2, R1, **X**, **▲**, **X**, **▲**, Up, Down

**Women with Guns**
Right, L1, **●**, L2, Left, **X**, R1, L1, L1, **X**

**Women Follow You**
**●**, **X**, L1, L1, R2, **X**, **X**, **●**, **▲**

**Media Level Meter**
R2, **●**, Up, L1, Right, R1, Right, Up, **■**, **▲**

## Weapon Cheats

The following will give you one weapon for each weapon class:

**Weapons Set 1**
R2, R2, R1, R2, L1, R2, Left, Down, Right, Up, Left Down, Right, Up

**Weapons Set 2**
R1, R2, L1, R2, Left, Down, Right, Up, Left, Down, Down, Left

**Weapons Set 3**
R1, R2, L1, R2, Left, Down, Right, Up, Left, Down, Down, Down

## Weather Cheats

Change the weather with the following cheats:

### Clear
R2, **X**, L1, L1, L2, L2, L2, Down

### Sunny
R2, **X**, L1, L1, L2, L2, L2, ▲

### Overcast
R2, **X**, L1, L1, L2, L2, L2, ■

### Rain
R2, **X**, L1, L1, L2, L2, L2, ●

### Fog
R2, **X**, L1, L1, L2, L2, L2, **X**

## Appearance Cheats

The following change your appearance to the indicated character:

### Red Leather
Right, Right, Left, Up, L1, L2, Left, Up, Down, Right

### Candy Suxxx
●, R2, Down, R1, Left, Right, R1, L1, **X**, L2

### Hilary King
R1, ●, R2, L1, Right, R1, L1, **X**, R2

### Ken Rosenberg
Right, L1, Up, L2, L1, Right, R1, L1, **X**, R1

### Lance Vance
●, L2, Left, **X**, R1, L1, **X**, L1

### Mercedes
R2, L1, Up, L1, Right, R1, Right, Up, ●, ▲

### Love Fist 1
Down, L1, Down, L2, Left, **X**, R1, L1, **X**, **X**

### Phil Cassady
Right, R1, Up, R2, L1, Right, R1, L1, Right, ●

### Love Fist 2
R1, L2, R2, L1, Right, R2, Left, **X**, ■, L1

### Ricardo Diaz
L1, L2, R1, R2, Down, L1, R2, L2

**Sonny Forelli**

●, L1, ●, L2, Left, **X**, R1, L1, **X**, **X**

## Vehicle Cheats

The following vehicles will drop from the sky:

**Bloodring Banger**

Up, Right, Right, L1, Right, Up, ■, L2

**Bloodring Banger**

Down, R1, ●, L2, L2, **X**, R1, L1, Left, Left

**Caddy**

●, L1, Up, R1, L2, **X**, R1, L1, ●, **X**

**Hotring Racer**

R2, L1, ●, Right, L1, R1, Right, Up, ●, R2

**Hotring Racer**

R1, ●, R2, Right, L1, L2, **X**, **X**, ■, R1

**Love Fist Limo**

R2, Up, L2, Left, Left, R1, L1, ●, Right

**Rhino Tank**

●, ●, L1, ●, ●, ●, ●, L1, L2, R1, ▲, ●, ▲

### Romero's Hearse

Down, R2, Down, R1, L2, Left, R1, L1, Left, Right

### Trashmaster

●, R1, ●, R1, Left, Left, R1, L1, ●, Right

### Sabre Turbo

Right, L2, Down, L2, L2, **X**, R1, L1, ●, Left

# HIGH HEAT MAJOR LEAGUE BASEBALL 2004

### Ball Cannon and Game State Options

Pause the game and press ■, ■, ●, ●, L1, R1. Then, press L1 + L2 + R1 + R2.

# HITMAN 2: SILENT ASSASSIN

### Level Select

At the main menu, press R2, L2, Up, Down, ■, ▲, ●.

## Complete Level

During a game, press R2, L2, Up, Down, **X**, L3, ●, **X**, ●, **X**.

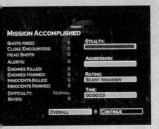

## All Weapons

During a game, press R2, L2, Up, Down, **X**, Up, ■, **X**.

## Invincibility

During a game, press R2, L2, Up, Down, **X**, R2, L2, R1, L1.

## Full Heal

During a game, press R2, L2, Up, Down, **X**, Up, Down.

## Toggle Lethal Charge

During a game, press R2, L2, Up, Down, **X**, R1, R1.

## Gravity

During a game, press R2, L2, Up, Down, **X**, L2, L2.

## Slow Motion

During a game, press R2, L2, Up, Down, **X**, Up, L2.

## Megaforce

During a game, press R2, L2, Up, Down, **X**, R2, R2.

## Toggle Bomb Mode

During a game, press R2, L2, Up, Down, **X**, Up, L1.

## Toggle Punch Mode

During a game, press R2, L2, Up, Down, **X**, Up, Up.

## Toggle Nailgun Mode

During a game, press R2, L2, Up, Down, **X**, L1, L1.

# HULK

## Cheat Codes

Select Code Input from the Options and enter the following and press Accept. Turn on the cheats by selecting Cheats from the Special Features menu.

| Description | Code Input |
| --- | --- |
| Invulnerability | GMMSKIN |
| Regenerator | FLSHWND |
| Unlimited Continues | GRNCHTR |

| Description | Code Input |
| --- | --- |
| Double Hulk HP | HLTHDSE |
| Double Enemies HP | BRNGITN |
| Half Enemies HP | MMMYHLP |
| Reset High Score | NMBTHIH |
| Full Rage Meter | ANGMNGT |
| Puzzle Solved | BRCESTN |
| Wicked Punch | FSTOFRY |
| Unlock All Levels | TRUBLVR |

### Universal Unlock Codes

Enter the following at the special terminals, called "Universal Code Input," that are found throughout the levels. You will find these bonus materials in the Special Features menu.

| Play as Gray Hulk | JANITOR |
| --- | --- |
| Desert Battle Art | FIFTEEN |
| Hulk Movie FMV Art | NANOMED |
| Hulk Transformed ART | SANFRAN |
| Hulk vs. Hulk Dogs Art | PITBULL |

# HUNTER: THE RECKONING WAYWARD

### Cheat List

Before using the following cheats, you must first defeat the game. While playing a game, enter the Enable Cheats code, then you can enter the rest.

| Effect | Code |
| --- | --- |
| Enable Cheats | ●, ■, ▲, X, LI, LI, Left, Left |
| Gain All Weapons | ■, X, ●, X, Up, Down, Up, Down |
| Improve Edges | LI, LI, ●, ●, Down, Down, Up, Down |
| Max Ammo | Right, Right, Right, Right, Up, Down, Up, Down |
| Max Health | ▲, ▲, ●, ●, ■, LI, ■, RI |
| Mega Melee Damage | Down, Down, RI, RI, Up, X, Up, ● |
| Monster Spawning On/Off | ■, ■, ●, ●, ▲, LI, LI |

| Effect | Code |
|---|---|
| No Conviction | L2, Up, **X**, Up, ■, Down, Down |
| | Cost for Edges |
| Tougher Monsters | ■, ■, ▲, ■, L2, L2, Up, Down |
| Unlimited Ammo | X, ▲, ●, ■, ▲, Up, Down, Down |
| Unlimited Life | Right, Right, Right, **X**, Up, ▲, Up, ■ |

# JAMES BOND 007: NIGHTFIRE

Select Codenames from the main menu and select your codename. Select Secret Unlocks and enter the following codes. Save your codename before backing out of this menu.

**Level Select**
Enter **PASSPORT**.

**Alpine Escape Level**
Enter **POWDER**.

**Enemies Vanquished Level**
Enter **TRACTION**.

**Double Cross Level**
Enter **BONSAI**.

**Night Shift Level**
Enter **HIGHRISE**.

**Chain Reaction Level**
Enter **MELTDown**.

**Phoenix Fire Level**
Enter **FLAME**.

**Deep Descent Level**
Enter **AQUA**.

**Island Infiltration Level**
Enter **PARADISE**.

**Countdown Level**
Enter **BLASTOFF**.

**Equinox Level**
Enter **VACUUM**.

**All Gadget Upgrades**
Enter **Q LAB**.

**Camera Upgrade**
Enter **SHUTTER**.

**Decrypter Upgrade**
Enter **SESAME**.

**Grapple Upgrade**
Enter **LIFTOFF**.

**Laser Upgrade**
Enter **PHOTON**.

**Scope Upgrade**
Enter **SCOPE**.

**Stunner Upgrade**
Enter **ZAP**.

**Tranquilizer Dart Upgrade**
Enter **SLEEPY**.

**Bigger Clip for Sniper Rifle**
Enter **MAGAZINE**.

**P2K Upgrade**
Enter **P2000**.

**Golden Wolfram P2K**
Enter **AU P2K**.

**Golden PP7**
Enter **AU PP7**.

**Vanquish Car Missile Upgrade**
Enter **LAUNCH**.

**All Multiplayer Scenarios**
Enter **GAMEROOM**.

**Uplink Multiplayer Scenario**
Enter **TRANSMIT**.

**Demolition Multiplayer Scenario**
Enter **TNT**.

**Protection Multiplayer Scenario**
Enter **GUARDIAN**.

**GoldenEye Strike Multiplayer Scenario**
Enter **ORBIT**.

**Assassination Multiplayer Scenario**
Enter **TARGET**.

**Team King of the Hill Multiplayer Scenario**
Enter **TEAMWORK**.

**Explosive Scenery Option in Multiplayer**
Enter **BOOM**. Find this option in the Enviro-Mods menu.

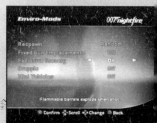

**Explosive Scenery Option in Multiplayer**

Enter **BOOM**. Find this option in the Enviro-Mods menu.

**All Characters in Multiplayer**

Enter **PARTY**.

**Play as Bond Tux in Multiplayer**

Enter **BLACKTIE**.

**Play as Drake Suit in Multiplayer**

Enter **NUMBER I**.

**Play as Bond Spacesuit in Multiplayer**

Enter **ZERO G**.

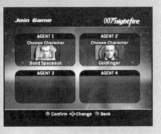

**Play as Goldfinger in Multiplayer**

Enter **MIDAS**.

**Play as Renard in Multiplayer**

Enter **HEADCASE**.

**Play as Scaramanga in Multiplayer**

Enter **ASSASSIN**.

**Play as Christmas Jones in Multiplayer**

Enter **NUCLEAR**.

**Play as Wai Lin in Multiplayer**

Enter **MARTIAL**.

**Play as Xenia Onatopp in Multiplayer**

Enter **JANUS**.

**Play as May Day in Multiplayer**

Enter **BADGIRL**.

**Play as Elektra King in Multiplayer**

Enter **SLICK**.

**Play as Jaws in Multiplayer**

Enter **DENTAL**.

**Play as Baron Samedi in Multiplayer**

Enter **VOODOO**.

**Play as Oddjob in Multiplayer**

Enter **BOWLER**.

**Play as Nick Nack in Multiplayer**

Enter **BITESIZE**.

**Play as Max Zorin in Multiplayer**

Enter **BLIMP**.

**Drive an SUV on Enemies Vanquished Level**

Start the Enemies Vanquished Level and pause the game. Hold L1 and press ■, ●, ▲, ■, ▲, then release L1.

**Race the Enemies Vanquished Level in Cobra**

Start the Enemies Vanquished Level and pause the game. Hold **L1** and press ●, ●, ■, ■, ▲, then release **L1**.

Enter the following during a driving level:

**Faster Racing**

Pause the game, hold **L1** and press ■, ▲, ●, ■, ▲, ●, then release **L1**.

**Berserk Racing**

Pause the game, hold **L1** and press ■, ▲, ▲, ■, ▲, ●, then release **L1**.

**Trails During Racing**

While racing on the Paris Prelude, Enemies Vanquished, Island Infiltration, or Deep Descent level, press START to pause game play, then hold **L1** and press ■, ●, ●, ■, then release **L1**.

### Double Armor During Racing

While racing on the Paris Prelude, Enemies Vanquished, Island Infiltration, or Deep Descent level, press START to pause game play, then hold **L1** and press ■, ▲, ●, ■, ■, then release **L1**.

### Triple Armor During Racing

While racing on the Paris Prelude, Enemies Vanquished, Island Infiltration, or Deep Descent level, press START to pause game play, then hold **L1** and press ■, ▲, ●, ■ (x3), then release **L1**.

### Quadruple Armor During Racing

While racing on the Paris Prelude, Enemies Vanquished, Island Infiltration, or Deep Descent level, press START to pause game play, then hold **L1** and press ■, ▲, ●, ■ (x4), then release **L1**.

### Super Bullets During Racing

While racing on the Paris Prelude, Enemies Vanquished, Island Infiltration, or Deep Descent level, press START to pause game play, then hold **L1** and press ● (x4), then release **L1**. Note: This can also be done when you are flying the plane with Alura.

# JURASSIC PARK: OPERATION GENESIS

### Gimme Some Money

During a game, press **L1**, Up, **L1**, Down, **L1**. This will give you $10,000.

### Where's the Money?

During a game, press **R1**, **L1**, Down. This will take all of your money away.

### Impossible Mission

During a game, press **R1**, Left, Left, Left, Left, **R1**. This will give you all missions complete.

### Rampage Time

During a game, press **L1**, **L1**, **L1**, Left, Left, Left. With this cheat, all carnivores will rampage.

### Extinction Event

During a game, press **L1**, **R1**, Down, **R1**, **L1**. This will kill all dinosaurs.

### Oh No!

During a game, hold **R1** and press Right, Left, Right, Left, Right. This will kill all visitors.

### Dial-A-Twister

During a game, press Left, Up, Right, Down, **L1**, **R1**.

### No Twisters

During a game, hold **L1** + **R1**, press Left, Right, then press **R1**, **L1**.

### Hot One

During a game, hold **R1** and press Down, Down. This will cause a heat wave.

### Welcome to Melbourne

During a game, press **R1**, **R1**, **L1**, **R1**, Down, Up, Down. This will cause rainstorms.

### Guaranteed Immunity

During a game, hold **L1** and press **R1**, Up, Up. Dinosaurs won't get sick with this cheat.

### No Red Tape

During a game, press **L1**, **R1**, Left, Down, Down, Down. With this cheat, you will not get charged for deaths.

### Open to the Public

During a game, press Left, Down, Right, Up, **L1**, **R1**, **L1**, **R1**. This gives you selection of dig sites without required stars.

### Market Day

During a game, press **R1**, **L1**, Down, **R1**, **L1**, Down.

### Sequencing Error

During a game, press Down, **R1**, Up. This gives 55% dinosaur genomes.

### Drive By

During a game, press **R1**, **L1**, Left, Down, Right, Right. Safari ride camera acts like a gun.

### Crash

During a game, old **R1** + **L1** and press Up, Down, Up, Down.

### Isla Muerta

During a game, press **R1**, **R1**, **R1**, **L1**, Right. Dinosaurs will appear decayed.

# MIDNIGHT CLUB II

Select Cheat Codes from the Options and enter the following:

 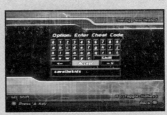

### All Vehicles

Enter theCollector.

### All Cities, Vehicles, and Career in Arcade Mode

Enter pennyThug or rimbuk.

### All Cities in Arcade Mode

Enter Globetrotter.

### Weapons

Enter savethekids. Use L3 and R3 to fire.

### Weapons and Invulnerable

Enter immortal.

### Unlimited Nitrous in Arcade Mode

Enter greenLantern.

## No Damage in Arcade Mode

Enter gladiator.

## Better Air Control

Enter carcrobatics.

## Change Difficulty

Enter one of the following. 0 is easiest, 9 is hardest.

*howhardcanitbe0*     *howhardcanitbe5*

*howhardcanitbe1*     *howhardcanitbe6*

*howhardcanitbe2*     *howhardcanitbe7*

*howhardcanitbe3*     *howhardcanitbe8*

*howhardcanitbe4*     *howhardcanitbe9*

# MINORITY REPORT

Select Cheats from the Special menu and enter the following

## Invincibility

Enter LRGARMS.

**Level Warp All**
Enter PASSKEY.

**Level Skip**
Enter QUITER.

**All Combos**
Enter NINJA.

**All Weapons**
Enter STRAPPED.

**Infinite Ammo**
Enter MRJUAREZ.

**Super Damage**
Enter SPINACH.

**Health**
Enter BUTTERUp.

Select Alternate Heroes from the Special menu to find the following:

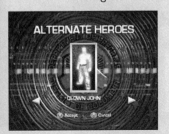

**Clown Hero**
Enter SCARYCLOWN.

**Convict Hero**
Enter JAILBREAK.

**GI John Hero**
Enter GNRLINFANTRY.

**Lizard Hero**
Enter HISSSS.

**Moseley Hero**
Enter HAIRLOSS.

**Nara Hero**
Enter WEIGHTGAIN.

**Nikki Hero**
Enter BIGLIPS.

**Robot Hero**
Enter MRROBOTO.

**Super John Hero**
Enter SUPERJOHN.

**Zombie Hero**
Enter IAMSODEAD.

**Free Aim**
Enter FPSSTYLE.

**Pain Arenas**
Enter MAXIMUMHURT.

**Armor**
Enter STEELUP.

**Baseball Bat**
Enter SLUGGER.

**Rag Doll**
Enter CLUMSY.

**Slomo Button**
Enter SLIZOMIZO.

**Bouncy Men**
Enter BOUNZMEN.

**Wreck the Joint**
Enter CLUTZ.

**Dramatic Finish**
Enter STYLIN.

**Ending**
Enter WIMP.

**Concept Art**
Enter SKETCHPAD.

**All Movies**
Enter DIRECTOR.

**Do Not Select**
Enter DONOTSEL.

# MLB 2004

**Big Ball**
Pause the game and press **L1**, **L2**, **L1**, **L2**, Up, Right, Down, Left.

**Big Bodies**
Pause the game and press Up, Down, Left, Right, **L1**, **L2**, **R2**, **R1**.

### No Bodies

Pause the game and press **R1**, **R2**, **R1**, **R2**, Up, Down, Left, Right.

### Small Heads

Pause the game and press Up, Down, Up, Down, **R1**, **R1**, **L1**, **L1**.

### Big Heads

Pause the game and press Up, Left, Down, Right, Up, Right, Down, Left.

### Fast Players

Pause the game and press Left, Right, Right, Left, **L1**, **R1**, **R1**, **L1**.

### Slow Players

Pause the game and press Left, Left, Right, Right, **R2**, **R2**, **L2**, **L2**.

### Programmer Names

Pause the game and press **R1**, **R2**, Right, Right, Left, Left, **L2**, **L1**.

# MLB SLUGFEST 20-04

### Cheats

At the Match-Up screen, use ■, ▲ and ● to enter the following codes, then press the appropriate direction. For example, for "16' Softball" press ■ two times, ▲ four times, ● two times, then press Down.

| Code | Enter |
| --- | --- |
| Cheats Disabled | 111 Down |
| Unlimited Turbo | 444 Down |
| 16' Softball | 242 Down |
| Whiffle Bat | 004 Right |

| Code | Enter |
| --- | --- |
| Whiffle Bat | 004 Right |

| Code | Enter |
| --- | --- |
| Big Head | 200 Right |
| Log Bat | 004 Up |

| Code | Enter |
| --- | --- |
| Ice Bat | 003 Up |
| Blade Bat | 002 Up |
| Spike Bat | 005 Up |
| Bone Bat | 001 Up |
| Coliseum Stadium | 333 Up |
| Rocket Park Stadium | 321 Up |
| Monument Stadium | 333 Down |

| Code | Enter |
| --- | --- |
| Midway Park Stadium | 321 Down |
| Empire Park Stadium | 321 Right |
| Forbidden City Stadium | 333 Left |

| Code | Enter |
| --- | --- |
| Atlantis Stadium | 321 Left |
| Rubber Ball | 242 Up |
| Mace Bat | 004 Left |
| Tiny Head | 200 Left |
| Max Batting | 300 Left |
| Max Power | 030 Left |
| Max Speed | 003 Left |
| Pinto Team | 210 Right |
| Horse Team | 211 Right |
| Eagle Team | 212 Right |
| Lion Team | 220 Right |

| | |
| --- | --- |
| Team Terry Fitzgerald | 333 Right |
| Team Todd McFarlane | 222 Right |
| Dwarf Team | 103 Down |
| Gladiator Team | 113 Down |
| Bobble Head Team | 133 Down |
| Dolphin Team | 102 Down |
| Scorpion Team | 112 Down |
| Rodeo Clown | 132 Down |
| Little League | 101 Down |
| Minotaur Team | 110 Down |
| Olshan Team | 222 Down |
| Rivera Team | 222 Up |
| Napalitano Team | 232 Down |

| Code | Enter |
|------|-------|
| Evil Clown Team | 211 Down |

| Alien Team | 231 Down |
| Casey Team | 233 Down |
| Extended Time For Codes | 303 Up |

# NASCAR: DIRT TO DAYTONA

## Master Code

At the title screen, press **R1**, **R1**, Up, Down, **R2**, **R2**, Left, Right.

# NASCAR THUNDER 2004

## All Cameos

Select Create-A-Car from the Features menu and name your car Seymore Cameos.

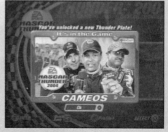

# NBA 2K3

### Codes

Select Game Play from the Options menu, hold Left on the D-pad + Right on the Left Analog Stick and press START. Back out to the Options, and a Codes option should appear.

### Sega Sports, Visual Concepts and NBA 2K3 Teams

Enter MEGASTARS as a code.

### Street Trash

Enter SPRINGER as a code.

# NBA LIVE 2003

Select Roster Management from the Team Management menu. Create a player with the following last names. These characters will be available as free agents.

### B-Rich

DOLLABILLS

## Busta Rhymes
FLIPMODE

## Hot Karl
CALIFORNIA

## DJ Clue
MIXTAPES

## Just Blaze
GOODBEATS

## Fabolous
GHETTOFAB

# NBA STREET VOL. 2

Select Pick Up Game, hold **L1** and enter the following when it says "Enter cheat codes now" at the bottom of the screen:

**Unlimited Turbo**
■, ■, ▲, ▲

**ABA Ball**
●, ■, ●, ■

**WNBA Ball**
Hold **L1** and press ●, ▲, ▲, ●

**No Display Bars**
■, ● (x3)

**All Jerseys**
■, ▲, ●, ●

**All Courts**
■, ▲, ▲, ■

**St. Lunatics Team and All Street Legends**
■, ▲, ●, ▲

### All NBA Legends
■, ▲, ▲, ●

### Classic Michael Jordan
■, ▲, ■ ■

### Explosive Rims
● (x3), ▲

### Hard Shots
▲, ■, ●, ▲

### Small Players
▲, ▲, ●, ■

### Big Heads
●, ■, ■, ●

### No Counters
▲, ▲, ●, ●

### Ball Trails
▲, ▲, ▲, ■

### All Quicks
▲, ●, ▲, ■

### Easy Shots
▲, ●, ■, ▲

# PRIMAL

## Magic Codes

At the Main, Options, or Bonus Materials menu, hold **L1** + **L2** + **R1** + **R2** until the Magic Codes menu appears. Hold **X** on a letter and press Left or Right to change that letter. Once you have entered one of the following, press ■ to accept the code. Press ▲ to go back to the previous menu.

| Invulnerable | MONSTROUS |
| Bonus B | PRIMAL |
| Bonus C | DEMONREALMS |
| Bonus E | OBLIVION |

# PRO RACE DRIVER

Enter the following codes at the Bonus screen:

### Realistic Handling

Enter SIM.

### Enhanced Damage

Enter DAMAGE.

### Credits

Enter CREDITS.

# RATCHET AND CLANK

Defeat Drek, and then at the Goodies screen do the following:

### Big Head Mode (Clank)

Flip Back, Hyper-Strike, Comet-Strike, Double Jump, Hyper-Strike, Flip Left, Flip Right, Full Second Crouch.

**Big Head Mode (Enemies)**

Stretch Jump, Flip Back, Flip Back, Flip Back, Stretch Jump, Flip Back, Flip Back, Flip Back, Stretch Jump, Flip Back, Flip Back, Flip Back, Full Second Crouch.

**Big Head Mode (Non-Player Characters)**

Flip Left, Flip Right, Flip Back, Flip Back, Comet-Strike, Double Jump, Comet-Strike, Hyper-Strike

**Big Head Mode (Ratchet)**

Flip Back, Flip Back, Flip Back, Full Second Crouch, Stretch Jump, Full Second Glide

**Health at Max Gives Temporary Invincibility**

Comet-Strike (x4), Flip Back, Full Second Crouch, Flip Back, Full Second Crouch, Comet-Strike (x4)

**Mirrored Levels**

Flip Left, Flip Left, Flip Left, Flip Left, 3-Hit Wrench Combo, Hyper Strike, Double Flip Right, Flip Right, Flip Right, Double Jump, Full Second Crouch

**Trippy Trails**

Wall Jump (x10), Double Jump, Hyper-Strike

## ROCKY

**Punch Double Damage**

At the main menu, hold **R1** and press Right, Down, Left, Up, Left, **L1**.

**Double Speed Boxing**

At the main menu, hold **R1** and press Down, Left, Down, Up, Right, **L1**.

### All Default Boxers, Arenas, and Rocky Statue

At the main menu, hold **R1** and press Right (x3), Left, Right, **L1**.

### All Default Boxers, Arenas, Rocky Statue, and Mickey

At the main menu, hold **R1** and press Up, Down, Down, Left, Left, **L1**.

### Full Stats In Tournament and Exhibition Modes

At the main menu, hold **R1** and press Left, Up, Up, Down, Right, **L1**.

### Full Stats in Movie Mode

At the main menu, hold **R1** and press Right, Down, Down, Up, Left, **L1**.

### Win Fight in Movie Mode

At the main menu, hold **R1** and press Right, Right, Left, Left, Up, **L1**. During a fight, press **R2** + **L2** to win.

# RTX RED ROCK

Pause the game, select Codes from the Options and enter the following:

### Level Select

Enter Down, Left, Left, Down, Left, Down, Right, Down, Left, Down. At the main menu, hold **R1** to access the Level Select.

### Add Items

Enter Right (x5), Left (x3), Up, Up.

### Old Soul Super Weapons

Enter Right, Up, Down, Down, Up, Right, Right, Up, Down, Down.

### Easy

Enter Up, Down (x8), Up.

### Normal Difficulty

Enter Up, Down, Up, Down, Up, Down, Up, Down, Up, Down.

### Difficult

Enter Down, Up (x8), Down.

### Special Features

Enter Left, Down, Up, Left, Right, Up, Down, Left, Right, Down.

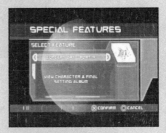

### Higher Quality Video

If you own a progressive scan television, enter Right, Up, Right, Right, Up, Right (x3), Up, Right.

# RUN LIKE HELL

## Cheats

At the inventory screen, press **L1** + **L2** + L3 + **R1** + **R2** + R3. Then enter the following:

| Effect | Code |
| --- | --- |
| Refill Health | Up, Down, Up, Down, Left, Right, Left, Right, **X**, ● |
| Refill Armor | ■, ●, **X**, ▲, ●, ■, ▲, **X**, L3, R3 |
| Music Video | Left, Left, Left, ●, ●, **X**, **L1**, **L1**, **R1**, Up |

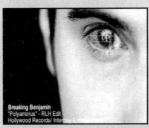

Breaking Benjamin
"Polyamorus" - RLH Edit
Hollywood Records/ Inter...

| Credits | **X**, ■, ▲, ●, Right, Up, Left, Up, **X**, Up |

| Max Damage (rifle) | L3, L3, L3, ■, ▲, ●, **X**, R3, R3, R3 |
| Max Damage (pulse) | Left, Right, ●, Down, Left, **X**, Down, Up, **X**, ▲ |
| Max Damage (shotgun) | **X**, **X**, **X**, **X**, L3, R3, Up, Down, Left, Right |
| Max Damage (repeater) | Left, ▲, Right, **X**, Up, ■, Down, ●, R3, L3 |
| Max Damage (assault) | Left, ●, Right, ■, Down, ▲, Up, **X**, L3, R3 |
| Max Damage (bolt toss) | **X**, ■, ▲, ●, **X**, ●, ▲, ■, **X**, Up |

# SHOX

## $2,500,000

Start a new game in single player mode and enter **LOADED** as a name.

# SILENT HILL 3

### Costumes

Beating the game on any Action Level entitles you to access the Extra Costume screen, using the option that is newly available on the title screen menu. You may enter letters to form passwords that unlock extra costumes. Once you type in a password correctly and press the red "Enter" button, the costume becomes unlocked. The extra costume becomes available in your Items inventory when you start your next game.

| Shirt | Password |
|-------|----------|
| "Block Head" | PutHere2FeelJoy |
| "Don't Touch" | TOUCH_MY_HEART |

| | |
|-------|----------|
| "Game Reactor" | SH3_Wrestlarn |
| "God of Thunder" | Shut_your_mouth |

| "Golden Rooster" | cockadooodledoo |
| "Heather" | HappyBirthDay |
| "Killer Rabbit" | BlueRobbieWin |

| "Onsen" | I_Love_You |
| "Play" | sLmLdGhSmKfBfH |

| EGM | EGMpretaporter |
| Gamepro | ProTip |
| Game Informer | gameinformer |
| GMR | GMRownzjoo |
| OPM | SH3_OPiuM |
| PSM | badical |
| "Royal Flush" | 01_03_08_11_12 |
| "The Light" | LightToFuture |
| Transform Costume | PrincessHeart |

"Transience"           ShogyouMujou

"Zipper"           Shut_your_mouth

## Douglas the Flasher

Complete the game to unlock the Extra New Game. On the title screen, highlight "Extra New Game" then press:

Up, Up, Down, Down, Left, Right, Left, Right, ●, **X**

Then select your desired Action and Riddle Levels, and Heather will make a strange noise. Throughout the game, Douglas refuses to wear a shirt or pants.

Sorry... I'll wait here.

# SIMPSONS SKATEBOARDING

At the character select, hold L1 + L2 + R1 + R2 and enter the following:

**All Boards**
Press **X**, ▲, ●, ■.

**Level Select**
Press ▲, **X**, ■, ●.

**99 Dollars**
Press ▲, **X**, ●, ■.

**All Skaters**
Press ●, ▲, **X**, ■.

**Fuzzy Skaters**
Press **X**, ▲, ■, ●.

**Big Head Homer**
Press ●, **X**, ▲, ■.

**Underwear Homer**
Press ▲, ●, **X**, ■.

**Big Head Bart**
Press **X**, ■, ●, ▲.

**Gangsta Bart**
Press ●, X, ■, ▲.

**Demon Marge**
Press X, ■, ▲, ●.

**Big Head Lisa**
Press ■, ▲, X, ●.

**Gangsta Lisa**
Press ■, ▲, ●, X.

**Big Head Nelson**
Press ▲, ■, ●, X.

**Ballerina Nelson**
Press ▲, ■, X, ●.

**Sunglasses Otto**
Press ■, X, ●, ▲.

**Big Head Frink**
Press ■, X, ▲, ●.

**Groovy Frink**
Press X, ●, ▲, ■.

**Business Suit Krusty**
Press ●, ▲, ■, X.

**Big Head Chief Wiggum**
Press X, ●, ■, ▲.

**Man Eater Wiggum**
Press ▲, ●, ■, X.

# SOCCER SLAM

**Max Power**
At the title screen, press
L1, R1, Left, Right, ■, ■.

**Infinite Turbo**
At the title screen, press
L1, R1, Right, Up, ●, ●.

**Big Heads**
At the title screen, press
R1, L1, Up, Up, ■, ■.

**Big Hit Mode**
At the title screen, press
L1, R1, Up, Up, ●, ■.

## Infinite Spotlight

At the title screen, press L1, R1, Down, Right, ■, ●.

## Old School Ball

At the title screen, press R1, Right, Left, Left, ■, ●.

## Eyeball Ball

At the title screen, press R1, Right, Down, Up, ●, ●.

## Black Box Ball

At the title screen, press R1, Left, Left, Down, ●, ●.

## Kids Play Ball

At the title screen, press R1, Right, Up, Down, ●, ■.

## Kids Block Ball

At the title screen, press R1, Left, Right, Right, ■, ■.

## Earth Ball

At the title screen, press R1, Right, Right, Left, ●, ●.

## Rusty Can Ball

At the title screen, press R1, Left, Up, Up, ■, ■.

## Beach Ball

At the title screen, press R1, Right, Right, Down, ■, ●.

## Crate Ball

At the title screen, press R1, Left, Down, Right, ■, ●.

## Eight Ball

At the title screen, press R1, Right, Up, Up, ■, ■.

## Rob Willock's Head Ball

At the title screen, press R1, Left, Up, Left, ■, ●.

## All Stadiums

At the title screen, press R1, R1, Right, Right, Up (x5), ●, ●.

### Alpen Castle Stadium

At the title screen, press Up (x3), Down, ●, ●.

### Jungle Stadium

At the title screen, press L1, R1, Up, Down, Left, Right, ●, ■.

### Atoll Stadium

At the title screen, press Up, Up, Left, Left, ■, ■.

### Reactor Stadium

At the title screen, press Up, Left, Left, Right, ●, ■.

### Riviera Ruins Stadium

At the title screen, press Up, Down, Down, Right, ■, ●.

### Oasis Stadium

At the title screen, press L1, R1, Up, Up, Down, Down, ●, ●.

### All Items

At the title screen, press Left, ●, Left, ●, Left.

# SPEED KINGS

Enter the following as your Handle:

## Lap Times – Unlock Grand Prix

Enter .LAPT18.

## All meets won

Enter .MEET6.

## Complete Driving Test

Enter .TEST9.

## Master Cheat

Enter borkbork as a name.

## Respect Points

Enter .Resp ##. Replace ## with the desired amount of respect.

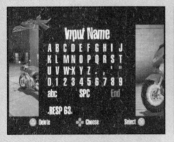

# STARSKY AND HUTCH

**Unlock Everything**

Enter VADKRAM as a profile name.

# SUMMER HEAT BEACH VOLLEYBALL

Select Game Settings from the Options, then select Cheats and enter the following:

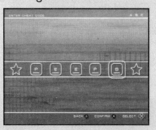

**All Characters**

Enter PEEPS.

**All Swimsuits and Shorts**

Enter GREED.

**All Accessories**
Enter WERIT.

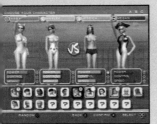

**All Locations**
Enter 80DAY.

**All Beach House Bonuses**
Enter MYPAD.

**All Mini Games**
Enter MAJOR.

**Hard and Expert Arcade Mode Difficulties**
Enter CHAMP.

**Sun Ball**
Enter HOT 1.

**Nerd Head Ball**
Enter GOLEM.

**Coconut Ball**
Enter MILKY.

**Disable Arrows**
Enter WHINE.

**Low Gravity**
Enter SPACE.

**Slow Motion Ball**
Enter ZIPPY.

**Nails Mode**
Enter NAILS.

**Spinning Heads**
Enter EXOSZ.

**Players with High Pitched Voices**
Enter MOUSE.

**Players with Low Pitched Voices**
Enter HORSE.

**All Videos**
Enter MUSAK.

**All Trailers**
Enter GAMON.

# TENCHU: WRATH OF HEAVEN

### All Characters

At the title screen, press L1, R2, L2, R1, Right, Left, L3, R3.

### All Story Mode Missions

At the Mission Select, press L1, R1, L2, R2, Right, ■, L3, R3.

### All Layouts

At the Mission Select, press R3, L3, R2, L2, R1, L1.

### All Multi-Player Missions

At the Mission Select, press L1, R1, L2, R2, Right, ■, L3, R3.

### Bonus Rikimaru stage

At the title screen, press L1, Up, R1, Down, L2, Right, R2, Left.

### Hidden level

At the title screen, press Up, Down, Right, Left, **X** (x3).

### All Items

At the Items screen, hold R1+L1 and press Up, ■, ■, Left, ■, ■, Down, ■, ■, Right, ■, ■.

### Increase Items

At the Items screen, hold R2 + L2 and press ■, ■, ■, Up, Left, Down, Right.

### Unlimited Item Capacity

At the Items screen, hold L1 + L2 + R1 + R2 and press ■ (x3), Up, Left, Down, Right, ■, Up, Right, Down, Left.

### Regain Health

Pause the game and press Up, Down, Right, Left, ■, ■, ■.

### Toggle Special Abilities

Pause the game, hold L1 + L2, and press Up, Up, Down, Down. Release L1 + L2 and press ■, ■, R1, R2.

### Add 100 Points

Pause the game, hold L1 + R1, and press Right, Right, Left, Left on controller two.

### Score and Time

Pause the game and press Right, Right, Left, Left on controller two.

## THE GETAWAY

Enter the following during the opening movie:

### Double Health

Press Up, Up, Left, Left, Right, Right, ●, ●, Down.

### Unlimited Ammo/No Reload

Press Up, Down, Left, Right, ▲, Up, Down, Left, Right, ■.

**Armored Car Weapon**

Press Up, Down, Left, Right, ■, ▲, ●. Use L3 to fire weapon.

**Free Roam Mode and Credits**

Press ▲ (x3), Left, ■, ▲ (x3), Left, ●.

# THE GREAT ESCAPE

**The Greatest Escape Mode and Select Level Option**

At the main menu, press ■, L2, ■, R2, ●, R1, ●, L1, L2, R2, ●, ■.

**Unlimited Ammo**

Pause the game and press ■, ●, L2, R1, R2, L1, ●, ■, L1, R1, L1, R1.

**Play All Movies**

At the main menu, press L2, L1, ■, ●, ●, R2, R1, ■, ■, ●, L1, R1. Press **X** to skip to next movie.

69

# THE LORD OF THE RINGS: THE TWO TOWERS

## Health

Pause the game, hold R1 + R2 + L1 + L2, and press ▲, Down, **X**, Up.

## Arrows

Pause the game, hold L1 + L2 + R1 + R2, and press **X**, Down, ▲, Up.

## 000 Experience Points

Pause the game, hold R1 + R2 + L1 + L2, and press **X**, Down(3).

## Level 2 Skills

Pause the game, hold R1 + R2 + L1 + L2, and press ●, Right, ●, Right.

## Level 4 Skills

Pause the game, hold R1 + R2 + L1 + L2, and press ▲, Up, ▲, Up.

## Level 6 Skills

Pause the game, hold R1 + R2 + L1 + L2, and press ■, Left, ■, Left.

## Level 8 Skills

Pause the game, hold R1 + R2 + L1 + L2, and press **X**, **X**, Down, Down.

Complete the game before entering the following codes:

### Always Devastating

Pause the game, hold R1 + R2 + L1 + L2, and press ■, ■, ●, ●.

### Small Enemies

Pause the game, hold R1 + R2 + L1 + L2, and press ▲, ▲, X, X.

### All Upgrades

Pause the game, hold R1 + R2 + L1 + L2, and press ▲, ●, ▲, ●.

### Invulnerable

Pause the game, hold R1 + R2 + L1 + L2, and press ▲, ■, X, ●.

### Slow Motion

Pause the game, hold R1 + R2 + L1 + L2, and press ▲, ●, X, ■.

### Unlimited Missile Weapons

Pause the game, hold R1 + R2 + L1 + L2, and press ■, ●, X, ▲.

# THE SIMPSONS: HIT & RUN

Select the Options from the main menu, hold L1 + R1 and enter the following:

### Invincible Car

Enter ▲, X, ▲, X.

### Red Brick Car

Enter ●, ●, ▲, ■.

### Fast Cars

Enter ■, ■, ■, ■.

### Faster Cars

Enter ▲, ▲, ▲, ▲.

### One-Hit Wreck

Enter ▲, ▲, ■, ■.

## Use Horn (L3) to Jump in Car

Enter ■, ■, ■, ▲.

## Show Speed

Enter ▲, ▲, ●, ■.

## Change Camera

Enter ●, ●, ●, X.

## Grid View

Enter ●, X, ●, ▲.

## Trippy

Enter ▲, ●, ▲, ●.

## Credits Dialog

Enter X, ■, ■, ▲.

## Holiday Decorated Living Room

Change the date of your system to Thanksgiving, Halloween or Christmas for a new look.

# THE SIMS

At the main menu, press L1 + R1 + L2 + R2, then enter
the following cheats:

### Play The Sims Mode, All 2-Player Games, Objects and Skins

Enter MIDAS. Select Get A Life and start a new game. Join
Roxy in the hot tub, pause the game and quit.

### All Objects Cost 0 Simoleans

Enter FREEALL.

### Party Motel Two-Player Game

Enter PARTY M.

### Play The Sims Mode
Enter SIMS.

### First Person View
Enter FISH EYE. Press ● to toggle the view.

# TIGER WOODS PGA TOUR 2004

Select Password from the Options menu and enter the following:

### All Golfers and Courses
Enter THEKITCHENSINK.

### All Courses
Enter ALLTHETRACKS.

### All Golfers
Enter CANYOUPICKONE

**Target® World Challenge**
Enter SHERWOOD TARGET.

**Sunday Tiger Woods**
Enter 4REDSHIRTS.

**Cedric "Ace" Andrews**
Enter ACEINTHEHOLE.

**Felicia "Downtown" Brown**
Enter DTBROWN.

**Dominic "The Don" Donatello**
Enter DISCOKING.

**Cedric The Entertainer**
Enter CEDDYBEAR.

**Solita Lopez**
Enter SHORTGAME.

**Edwin "Pops" Masterson**
Enter EDDIE.

**Hamish "Mulligan" McGregor**
Enter DWILBY.

**Takeharu "Tsunami" Moto**
Enter EMERALDCHAMP.

**Kellie Newman**
Enter TRAVELER.

**Val "Sunshine" Summers**
Enter BEVERLYHILLS.

**Moa "Big Mo" Ta'a Vatu**
Enter ERUPTION.

**Melvin "Yosh" Tanigawa**
Enter THENEWLEFTY.

**Erika "Ice" Von Severin**
Enter ICYONE.

# TOM AND JERRY: WAR OF THE WHISKERS

**Unlimited Health**
Press **X**, ●, **X**, ▲, ▲, ■, ●, ▲.

**Unlimited Ammunition**
Press ●, ■, ●, ▲, **X**, ■, **X**, **X**.

# TOMB RAIDER: THE ANGEL OF DARKNESS

**Skip Level and Level Select**
Pause the game, hold L1 + R2 + Down + ▲, release and press ●, Up, ■, ▲, Right, Down.

# TONY HAWK'S PRO SKATER 4

### All Cheats

Select Cheat Codes from the Options and enter **watch_me_xplode**.

### Eddie, Jango Fett and Mike Vallely

Select Cheat Codes from the Options and enter **homielist**.

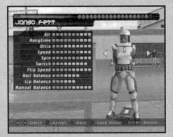

### Daisy

Select Cheat Codes from the Options and enter **(o)(o)**.

### Always Special

Select Cheat Codes from the Options and enter **doasuper**.

### Perfect Manuals

Select Cheat Codes from the Options and enter **mullenpower**.

### Perfect Rail

Select Cheat Codes from the Options and enter **ssbsts**.

### Matrix Mode

Select Cheat Codes from the Options and enter **nospoon**.

## Moon Gravity

Select Cheat Codes from the Options and enter **superfly**.

## Secret Created Skaters

Enter the following names for hidden created skaters:

#$%@!

Aaron Skillman

Adam Lippmann

Andrew Skates

Andy Marchal

Angus

Atiba Jefferson

Ben Scott Pye

Big Tex

Brian Jennings

Captain Liberty

Chauwa Steel

Chris Peacock

ConMan

Danaconda

Dave Stohl

DDT

DeadEndRoad

Fritz

Gary Jesdanun

grjost

Henry Ji

Jason Uyeda

Jim Jagger

Joe Favazza

John Rosser

Jow

Kenzo

Kevin Mulhall

Kraken

Lindsey Hayes

Lisa G Davies

Little Man

Marilena Rixfor

Mat Hoffman

Matt Mcpherson

Maya's Daddy

Meek West

Mike Day

Mike Lashever

Mike Ward

Mr. Brad

Nolan Nelson

Parking Guy

Peasus

Pete Day

Pooper

Rick Thorne

Sik

Stacey D

Stacey Ytuarte

Team Chicken

Ted Barber

Todd Wahoske

Top Bloke

Wardcore

Zac ZiG Drake

# WAKEBOARDING UNLEASHED

At the main menu, enter the following. You will get the corresponding message when entered correctly.

## All Gaps (gap kings)

Message: WAKEBOARDING ROYALTY

R1,L1,L2,R2, R1,L1,L2,R2, R1,L1,L2,R2, R1,L1,L2,R2

## Boards 2 and 3

Message: YOU GOT ALL THE BOARDS ...OR DID YOU

Up, Up, Left, Left, Right, Right, Down, Down, Up, Left, Right, Down, Up, Left, Right, Down

## All Levels

Message: TRAVEL VISA APPROVED

■, ■, ■, ■, ●, ●, ●, ●, ▲, ▲, ▲, ▲, ■, ●, ▲

# WHIRL TOUR

### All Characters and Levels

Press ▲, ■, ●, ▲, Down, Right, Up, Left, L1, L1, Right, Right, Down, Up, R1, ●, Left, ■, ■, Down.

### All Default Levels

Press ■ (x3), L1, Right, Down, ▲, Up, Left, ●, ■, Down, Up, R1, L1, Down, Down.

### All Bonus Levels

Press Up, Up, Down, Down, Left, Right, Left, Right, ■, ●, ▲.

### All Race Levels

Press ■, ▲, ●, ■, L1, ●, R1, ▲, L1, ●, R1, ■.

### All Extras Options

Press Left, Right, L1, R1, Down, Up, Right, Down, ●, ●, ▲, Right, R1.

### Complete All Current Objectives

Press ●, ●, ■, ●, ●, ▲, ●, ●, L1, R1.

# WHITEOUT

### All Characters

At the main menu, hold R1 + L1 and press Down, Down, Down, Down.

### All Tracks, Snowmobiles and Riders

At the main menu, hold R1 + L1 and press Right, Right, Right, Right.

### All Courses

At the main menu, hold R1 + L1 and press Up, Up, Up, Up.

### All Parts

At the main menu, hold L1 + R1 and press Left, Left, Left, Left.

### 10,000 Points

During a race, hold L2 + ▲ and press Right, Right, Up, Down.

### Automatically Win Race

During a race, hold L2 + ▲ and press Up, Down, Left, Right.

### Stamina Cheat

During a race, hold L2 + ▲ and press Right, Right, Left, Down.

### Target Cheat

During a race, hold L2 + ▲ and press Down, Down, Left, Left.

# X2: WOLVERINE'S REVENGE

### Level Select and All Challenges

At the main menu, press ▲, ●, ▲, ■, ▲, ●, LI + RI.

### All Costumes

At the main menu, press ▲, ●, ▲, ■, ■, ■, LI + L2.

### All Cerebro Files and FMV Sequences

At the main menu, press ▲, ●, ▲, ■, ■, ■, RI + R2.

### Cheats

At the main menu, press ▲, ▲, ●, ●, ■, ■, ●, ●, LI + RI + L2 + R2.

# YU-GI-OH! THE DUELIST OF THE ROSES

### Passwords

At the Build Deck screen, press R3 and enter the following passwords:

| Number | Card | Password |
|--------|------|----------|
| #001 | Seiyaryu | 2H4D85J7 |
| #019 | Meteor Dragon | 86985631 |
| #042 | Fairy's Gift | NVE7A3EZ |
| #043 | Magician of Faith | GMEIS3UM |
| #057 | Left Arm of the Forbidden One | A5CF6HSH |
| #058 | Exodia the Forbidden One | 37689434 |
| #146 | Swordstalker | AH0PSHEB |
| #149 | Greenkappa | YBJMCD6Z |
| #152 | Tactical Warrior | 054TC727 |
| #191 | Swordsman from a Foreign Land | CZ8IUVGR |

| Number | Card | Password |
|--------|------|----------|
| #478 | Aqua Dragon | JXCB6FU7 |
| #655 | Ancient Tree of Enlightenment | EKJHQ109 |
| #502 | Barrel Dragon | GTJXSBJ7 |
| #567 | Beastking of the Swamps | QXNTQPAX |
| #291 | Birdface | N54T4TY5 |
| #348 | Dragon Seeker | 8IEZCH8B |
| #372 | Mystical Capture Chains | NINDJMQ3 |
| #458 | Serpentine Princess | UMQ3WZUZ |
| #506 | Blast Sphere | CZN5GD2X |
| #510 | Robotic Knight | S5S7NKNH |
| #670 | Fairy King Truesdale | YF07QVEZ |
| #674 | Slate Warrior | 73153736 |
| #687 | Mimicat | 69YDQM85 |
| #699 | Dark Hole | UMJ10MQB |
| #702 | Harpy's Feather Duster | 8HJHQPNP |
| #732 | Change of Heart | SBYDQM8B |
| #750 | Earthshaker | Y34PN1SV |
| #758 | Elf's Light | E5G3NRAD |
| #765 | Horn of the Unicorn | S14FGKQ1 |
| #794 | Crush Card | SRA7L5YR |
| #806 | Gravity Bind | 0HNFG9WX |
| #814 | Goblin Fan | 92886423 |
| #825 | Royal Decree | 8TETQHEI |
| #829 | Mirror Wall | 53297534 |

# ZONE OF THE ENDERS: THE 2ND RUNNER

### Zoradius Mini Game

Fight Vic Viper in Boss Battle Mode. Pause the game and press Up, Up, Down, Down, Left, Right, Left, Right, L1, R1. The Mini Game will be available at the Extra Missions screen.

All Power-Ups in Zoradius Mini Game: All Power-Ups

Pause the game and press Up, Up, Down, Down, Left, Right, Left, Right, L1, R1.

# Games List

C-12: FINAL RESISTANCE . . . . . . . . . . . . . . . . . . . . . . .84

FINAL FANTASY ORIGINS . . . . . . . . . . . . . . . . . . . .85

STREAK: HOVERBOARD RACING . . . . . . . . . . . . . .85

STUART LITTLE 2 . . . . . . . . . . . . . . . . . . . . . . . . . .86

THE ITALIAN JOB . . . . . . . . . . . . . . . . . . . . . . . . . .86

TOMB RAIDER CHRONICLES . . . . . . . . . . . . . . . . . .87

TONY HAWK'S PRO SKATER 4 . . . . . . . . . . . . . . . .88

YU-GI-OH! FORBIDDEN MEMORIES . . . . . . . . . . . .88

# C-12: FINAL RESISTANCE

### Invincible

Pause the game, hold L2, and press Up, Left, Down, Right, ▲, ■, X, ●.

### All Weapons

Pause the game, hold L2, and press Up, Left, Right, Down, ▲, ■, ●, X.

### Shield

Pause the game, hold L2, and press Up, Left, Right, ▲, ■, ●.

### Infinite Ammo

Pause the game, hold L2, and press Down, Left, Right, X, ■, ●.

### Secondary Weapon Attacks

Pause the game, hold L2, and press Up, Down, Left, Right, ▲, X, ■, ●.

### Stealth Mode

Pause the game, hold L2, and press X, X, ■, ■, ▲, ▲, ●, ●, X, X.

# FINAL FANTASY ORIGINS

## FINAL FANTASY

### The Tile Game

When you're on your ship, hold **X**, then press ● 55 times to bring up a sliding tile puzzle game called 15 Puzzle. The game tracks your best time and rewards you accordingly:

Under 4 Minutes: Antidote and Potion

Under 2 Minutes: Golden Needle, Antidote, and Potion

1st Place Finish: 10,000 Gil

2nd Place Finish: 5,000 Gil

3rd Place Finish: 2,000 Gil

## FINAL FANTASY 2

### Concentration Mini Game

After you obtain the Snowcraft, hold **X** and press ● 15-20 times to start a game of concentration. An easy way to earn the maximum reward of 40,000 Gil, an Elixir, and a Phoenix Down, is to beat the first puzzle and note the locations of the pairs. Restart and quit the game 31 times. (Don't exit the game screen; just cancel immediately after starting a game.) Then, the thirty-second layout is the same as the first board.

# STREAK: HOVERBOARD RACING

### All Riders

Select Sierra for Freestyle in a 6 lap Time Trial. Besides Edge as blade 2, turn off other blades and start the race. Pause and quit the race. Then at the rider select, press ▲ and press Up, Down, L1, R2, R1, L2, ●, SELECT.

# STUART LITTLE 2

**Debug**

At the main menu, press Left, L1, L1, Right, R1, R1, Up, Down.

**Invincibility**

At the main menu, press L2, ■, L1, ●, R2, ■, L1, ●.

**Full Ammo**

At the main menu, ■, L1, R1, Up, ●, L2, R2, Down.

**Level Select**

At the main menu, press R2, Left, Right, R1, L1, Up, Down, L2.

**Flycam**

At the main menu, press Up, L1, Down, R1, R2, Down, L2, Up.

**All Movies**

At the main menu, press Right, ●, ■, ■, R1, R2, Left, L2.

**Gallery Movies**

At the main menu, press ●, L2, Left, R1, R2, Right, L1.

**Infinite Lives**

Pause the game, hold L1, and press ●, ●, ▲.

# THE ITALIAN JOB

Enter the following at the main menu, unless otherwise noted. Applause will indicate correct entry.

**All Cheats**

Press ▲, ●, ▲, ●, ▲, ■, ▲, ■.

**All Missions in Italian Job Mode**

Press ●, ●, ▲, ■, ■.

**All Missions in Challenge Mode**

Press ■, ■, ▲, ●, ●, ■, ▲, ●.

**All Missions in Checkpoint Mode**

Press ●, ■, ▲, ■, ▲, ■, ▲, ■, ●.

**All Missions in Destructor Mode**

Press ▲, ■, ■, ▲, ■, ■, ▲, ● (x3).

**All Missions in Free Ride**

Press ■, ▲, ■, ● (x3), ▲, ●.

**Level Select**

In Career mode, pause the game, hold **R1** and press ▲, Left, Left, ▲, ●, Up, Up, ■.

# TOMB RAIDER CHRONICLES

### Unlimited Health, Ammo, and Weapons

While in the game, press Select to access your inventory screen. Highlight the Timex and enter the following secret code:

Hold Up + R1 + L1 + L2 + R2 then press ▲.

### Every Item for Your Level

While in the game, press Select to access your inventory screen. Highlight the Timex and enter the following secret code:

Hold Down + R1 + L1 + L2 + R2 then press ▲.

This also gives you the Special Features option at the main menu.

### Start at Second Adventure

Highlight the New Game option at the main menu and enter the following secret code:

Hold L1 + Up then press **X** to start at the Russian Base.

### Start at Third Adventure

Highlight the New Game option at the main menu and enter the following secret code:

Hold L2 + Up then press **X** to start at the Black Isle.

### Start at Fourth Adventure

Highlight the New Game option at the main menu and enter the following secret code:

Hold R1 + Up then press **X** to start at the Tower Block.

# TONY HAWK'S PRO SKATER 4

### Complete Current Objective

Pause the game, hold L1, and press ▲, Right, Up, **X**, Right, ●, Up, ▲, ■, Left, Up, **X**.

# YU-GI-OH! FORBIDDEN MEMORIES

### Passwords

| Number | Card | Password |
|--------|------|----------|
| 001 | Blue Eyes White Dragon | 89631139 |
| 002 | Mystical Elf | 15025844 |
| 003 | Hitotsu-Me Giant | 76184692 |
| 004 | Baby Dragon | 88819587 |
| 005 | Ryu-Kishin | 15303296 |
| 006 | Feral Imp | 41392891 |
| 007 | Winged Dragon #1 | 87796900 |
| 008 | Mushroom Man | 14181608 |
| 009 | Shadow Specter | 40575313 |
| 010 | Blackland Fire Dragon | 87564352 |
| 011 | Sword Arm of Dragon | 13069066 |
| 012 | Swamp Battleguard | 40453765 |
| 013 | Tyhone | 72842870 |
| 014 | Battle Steer | 18246479 |
| 015 | Flame Swordsman | 45231177 |
| 016 | Time Wizard | 71625222 |
| 017 | Right Leg of the Forbidden One | 08124921 |

| Number | Card | Password |
|--------|------|----------|
| 018 | Left Leg of the Forbidden One | 44519536 |
| 019 | Right Arm of the Forbidden One | 70903634 |
| 020 | Left Arm of the Forbidden One | 07902349 |
| 021 | Exodia the Forbidden | 33396948 |
| 022 | Summoned Skull | 70781052 |
| 023 | The Wicked Worm Beast | 06285791 |
| 024 | Skull Servant | 32274490 |
| 025 | Horn Imp | 69669405 |
| 026 | Battle Ox | 05053103 |
| 027 | Beaver Warrior | 32452818 |
| 028 | Rock Ogre Grotto #1 | 68846917 |
| 029 | Mountain Warrior | 04931562 |
| 030 | Zombie Warrior | 31339260 |
| 031 | Koumori Dragon | 67724379 |
| 032 | Two-headed King Rex | 94119974 |
| 033 | Judgeman | 30113682 |
| 034 | Saggi the Dark Clown | 66602787 |
| 035 | Dark Magician | 46986414 |
| 036 | The Snake Hair | 29491031 |
| 037 | Gaia the Dragon Champion | 66889139 |
| 038 | Gaia the Fierce Knight | 06368038 |
| 039 | Curse of Dragon | 28279543 |
| 040 | Dragon Piper | 55763552 |
| 041 | Celtic Guardian | 91152256 |
| 042 | Illusionist Faceless Mage | 28546905 |
| 043 | Karbonala Warrior | 54541900 |
| 044 | Rogue Doll | 91939608 |
| 045 | Oscillo Hero #2 | 27324313 |
| 046 | Griffore | 53829412 |
| 047 | Torike | 80813021 |
| 048 | Sangan | 26202165 |
| 049 | Big Insect | 53606874 |
| 050 | Basic Insect | 89091579 |
| 051 | Armored Lizard | 15480588 |
| 052 | Hercules Beatle | 52584282 |
| 053 | Killer Needle | 88979991 |
| 054 | Gokibore | 15367030 |
| 055 | Giant Flea | 41762634 |
| 056 | Larvae Moth | 87756343 |
| 057 | Great Moth | 14141448 |
| 058 | Kuriboh | 40640057 |
| 059 | Mammoth Graveyard | 40374923 |
| 060 | Great White | 13429800 |

| Number | Card | Password |
|--------|------|----------|
| 061 | Wolf | 49417509 |
| 062 | Harpie Lady | 76812113 |
| 063 | Harpie Lady Sisters | 12206212 |
| 064 | Tiger Axe | 49791927 |
| 065 | Silver Fang | 90357090 |
| 066 | Kojikocy | 01184620 |
| 067 | Perfectly Ultimate Great Moth | 48579379 |
| 068 | Garoozis | 14977074 |
| 069 | Thousand Dragon | 41462083 |
| 070 | Fiend Kraken | 77456781 |
| 071 | Jellyfish | 14851496 |
| 072 | Cocoon of Evolution | 40240595 |
| 073 | Kairyu-Shin | 76634149 |
| 074 | Giant Soldier of Stone | 13039848 |
| 075 | Man-Eating Plant | 49127943 |
| 076 | Krokodilus | 76512652 |
| 077 | Grappler | 02906250 |
| 078 | Axe Raider | 48305365 |
| 079 | Megazowler | 75390004 |
| 080 | Uraby | 01784619 |
| 081 | Crawling Dragon #2 | 38289717 |
| 082 | Red-eyes B. Dragon | 74677422 |
| 083 | Castle of Dark Illusions | 00062121 |
| 084 | Reaper of the Cards | 33066139 |
| 085 | King of Yamimakai | 69455834 |
| 086 | Barox | 06840573 |
| 087 | Dark Chimera | 32344688 |
| 088 | Metal Guardian | 68339286 |
| 089 | Catapult Turtle | 95727991 |
| 090 | Gyakutenno Megami | 31122090 |
| 091 | Mystic Horseman | 68516705 |
| 092 | Rabid Horseman | 94905343 |
| 093 | Zanki | 30090452 |
| 094 | Crawling Dragon | 67494157 |
| 095 | Crass Clown | 93889755 |
| 096 | Armored Zombie | 20277860 |
| 097 | Dragon Zombie | 66672569 |
| 098 | Clown Zombie | 92667214 |
| 099 | Pumpking the King of Ghosts | 29155212 |
| 100 | Battle Warrior | 55550921 |
| 101 | Wings of Wicked Flames | 92944626 |
| 102 | Dark Mask | 28933734 |
| 103 | Job Change Mirror | 55337339 |

| Number | Card | Password |
|--------|------|----------|
| 104 | Curtain of the Dark Ones | 22026707 |
| 105 | Tomozaurus | 46457856 |
| 106 | Spirit of the Winds | 54615781 |
| 107 | Kagenigen | 80600490 |
| 108 | Graveyard and the Hand of Invitation | 27094595 |
| 109 | Goddess With the Third Eye | 53493204 |
| 110 | Hero of the East | 89987208 |
| 111 | Doma the Angel of Silence | 16972957 |
| 112 | The Witch that Feeds on Life | 52367652 |
| 113 | Dark Gray | 09159938 |
| 114 | White Magical Hat | 15150365 |
| 115 | Kamion Wizard | 41544074 |
| 116 | Nightmare Scorpion | 88643173 |
| 117 | Spirit of the Books | 14037717 |
| 118 | Supporter in the Shadows | 41422426 |
| 119 | Trial of Nightmares | 77827521 |
| 120 | Dream Clown | 13215230 |
| 121 | Sleeping Lion | 40200834 |
| 122 | Yamatano Dragon Scroll | 76704943 |
| 123 | Dark Plant | 13193642 |
| 124 | Ancient Tool | 49587396 |
| 125 | Faith Bird | 75582395 |
| 126 | Orion the Battle King | 02971090 |
| 127 | Ansatsu | 48365709 |
| 128 | Lamoon | 75850803 |
| 129 | Nemuriko | 90963488 |
| 130 | Weather Control | 37243151 |
| 131 | Octoberser | 74637266 |
| 132 | The 13th Grave | 00032864 |
| 133 | Charubin the Fire Knight | 37421579 |
| 134 | Mystical Capture Chain | 63515678 |
| 135 | Fiend's Hand | 52800428 |
| 136 | Witty Phantom | 36304921 |
| 137 | Mystery Hand | 62793020 |
| 138 | Dragon Statue | 09197735 |
| 139 | Blue-eyed Silver Zombie | 35282433 |
| 140 | Toad Master | 62671448 |
| 141 | Spiked Snail | 98075147 |
| 142 | Flame Manipulator | 34460851 |
| 143 | Necrolancer the Timelord | 61454890 |
| 144 | Djinn the Watcher of the Wind | 97843505 |
| 145 | The Bewitching Phantom Thief | 24348204 |
| 146 | Temple of Skulls | 00732302 |

| Number | Card | Password |
|--------|------|----------|
| 147 | Monster Egg | 36121917 |
| 148 | The Shadow Who Controls the Dark | 63125616 |
| 149 | Lord of the Lamp | 99510761 |
| 150 | Akihiron | 36904469 |
| 151 | Rhaintumdos of the Red Sword | 62403074 |
| 152 | The Melting Red Shadow | 98898173 |
| 153 | Dokuroize the Grim Reaper | 25882881 |
| 154 | Fire Reaper | 53581214 |
| 155 | Larvas | 94675535 |
| 156 | Hard Armor | 20060230 |
| 157 | Firegrass | 53293545 |
| 158 | Man Eater | 93553943 |
| 159 | Dig Beak | 29948642 |
| 160 | M-Warrior #1 | 56342351 |
| 161 | M-Warrior #2 | 92731455 |
| 162 | Tainted Wisdom | 28725004 |
| 163 | Lisark | 55210709 |
| 164 | Lord of Zemia | 81618817 |
| 165 | The Judgement Hand | 28003512 |
| 166 | Mysterious Puppeteer | 54098121 |
| 167 | Ancient Jar | 81492226 |
| 168 | Darkfire Dragon | 17881964 |
| 169 | Dark King of the Abyss | 53375573 |
| 170 | Spirit of the Harp | 80770678 |
| 171 | Big Eye | 16768387 |
| 172 | Armaill | 53153481 |
| 173 | Dark Prisoner | 89558090 |
| 174 | Hurricail | 15042735 |
| 175 | Ancient Brain | 42431843 |
| 176 | Fire Eye | 88435542 |
| 177 | Monsturtle | 15820147 |
| 178 | Claw Reacher | 41218256 |
| 179 | Phantom Dewan | 77603950 |
| 180 | Arlownay | 14708569 |
| 181 | Dark Shade | 40196604 |
| 182 | Masked Clown | 77581312 |
| 183 | Lucky Trinket | 03985011 |
| 184 | Genin | 49370026 |
| 185 | Eyearmor | 64511793 |
| 186 | Fiend Reflection #2 | 02863439 |
| 187 | Gate Deeg | 49258578 |
| 188 | Synchar | 75646173 |
| 189 | Fusionist | 01641882 |

| Number | Card | Password |
|--------|------|----------|
| 190 | Akakieisu | 38035986 |
| 191 | Lala Li-Oon | 09430387 |
| 192 | Key Mace | 01929294 |
| 193 | Turtle Tiger | 37313348 |
| 194 | Terra the Terrible | 63308047 |
| 195 | Doron | 36151751 |
| 196 | Arma Knight | 00756652 |
| 197 | Mech Mole Zombie | 63545455 |
| 198 | Happy Lover | 99030164 |
| 199 | Penguin Knight | 36039163 |
| 200 | Petit Dragon | 75356564 |
| 201 | Frenzied Panda | 98818516 |
| 202 | Air Marmot of Nefariousness | 75889523 |
| 203 | Phantom Ghost | 61201220 |
| 204 | Mabarrel | 98795934 |
| 205 | Dorover | 24194033 |
| 206 | Twin Long Rods #1 | 60589682 |
| 207 | Droll Bird | 97973387 |
| 208 | Petit Angel | 38142739 |
| 209 | Winged Cleaver | 39175982 |
| 210 | Hinotama Soul | 96851799 |
| 211 | Kaminarikozou | 15510988 |
| 212 | Meotoko | 53832650 |
| 213 | Aqua Madoor | 85639257 |
| 214 | Kagemusha of the Blue Flame | 15401633 |
| 215 | Flame Ghost | 58528964 |
| 216 | Dryad | 84916669 |
| 217 | B. Skull Dragon | 11901678 |
| 218 | Two-Mouth Darkruler | 57305373 |
| 219 | Solitude | 84794011 |
| 220 | Masked Sorcerer | 10189126 |
| 221 | Kumootoko | 56283725 |
| 222 | Midnight Fiend | 83678433 |
| 223 | Roaring Ocean Snake | 19066538 |
| 224 | Trap Master | 46461247 |
| 225 | Fiend Sword | 22855882 |
| 226 | Skull Stalker | 54844990 |
| 227 | Hitodenchak | 46718686 |
| 228 | Wood Remains | 17733394 |
| 229 | Hourglass of Life | 08783685 |
| 230 | Rare Fish | 80516007 |
| 231 | Wood Clown | 17511156 |
| 232 | Madjinn Gunn | 43905751 |

| Number | Card | Password |
|--------|------|----------|
| 233 | Dark Titan of Terror | 89494469 |
| 234 | Beautiful Head Huntress | 16899564 |
| 235 | Wodan the Resident of the Forest | 42883273 |
| 236 | Guardian of the Labyrinth | 89272878 |
| 237 | Haniwa | 84285623 |
| 238 | Yashinoki | 41061625 |
| 239 | Vishwar Randi | 78556320 |
| 240 | The Drdek | 08944575 |
| 241 | Dark Assassin | 41949033 |
| 242 | Candle of Fate | 47695416 |
| 243 | Water Element | 03732747 |
| 244 | Dissolverock | 40826495 |
| 245 | Meda Bat | 76211194 |
| 246 | One Who Hunts Souls | 03606209 |
| 247 | Root Water | 39004808 |
| 248 | Master & Expert | 75499502 |
| 249 | Water Omotics | 02483611 |
| 250 | Hyo | 38982356 |
| 251 | Enchanting Mermaid | 75376965 |
| 252 | Nekogal #1 | 01761063 |
| 253 | Angelwitch | 37160778 |
| 254 | Embryonic Beast | 64154377 |
| 255 | Prevent Rat | 00549481 |
| 256 | Dimensional Warrior | 37043180 |
| 257 | Stone Armadiller | 63432835 |
| 258 | Beastking of the Swamp | 99426834 |
| 259 | Ancient Sorcerer | 36821538 |
| 260 | Lunar Queen Elzaim | 62210247 |
| 261 | Wicked Mirror | 15150371 |
| 262 | The Little Swordsman of Aile | 25109950 |
| 263 | Rock Ogre Grotto #2 | 62193699 |
| 264 | Wing Egg Elf | 98582704 |
| 265 | The Furious Sea King | 18710707 |
| 266 | Princess of Tsurugi | 51371017 |
| 267 | Unknown Warrior of Fiend | 97360116 |
| 268 | Sectarian of Secrets | 15507080 |
| 269 | Versago the Destroyer | 50259460 |
| 270 | Wetha | 96643568 |
| 271 | Megirus Light | 23032273 |
| 272 | Mavelus | 59036972 |
| 273 | Ancient Tree of Enlightenment | 86421986 |
| 274 | Green Phantom King | 22910685 |
| 275 | Ground Attacker Bugroth | 58314394 |

| Number | Card | Password |
|--------|------|----------|
| 276 | Ray & Temperature | 85309439 |
| 277 | Gorgon Egg | 11793047 |
| 278 | Petit Moth | 58192742 |
| 279 | King Fog | 84686841 |
| 280 | Protector of the Throne | 10071456 |
| 281 | Mystic Clown | 47060154 |
| 282 | Mystical Sheep #2 | 83464209 |
| 283 | Holograph | 10859908 |
| 284 | Tao the Chanter | 46247516 |
| 285 | Serpent Maurauder | 82742611 |
| 286 | Gate Keeper | 19737320 |
| 287 | Ogre of the Black Shadow | 45121025 |
| 288 | Dark Arts | 72520073 |
| 289 | Change Slime | 18914778 |
| 290 | Moon Envoy | 45909477 |
| 291 | Fireyarou | 71407486 |
| 292 | Psychic Kappa | 07892180 |
| 293 | Masaki the Legendary Swordsman | 44287299 |
| 294 | Dragoness the Wiched Knight | 70681994 |
| 295 | Bio Plant | 07670542 |
| 296 | One-Eyed Shield Dragon | 33064647 |
| 297 | Cyber Soldier of Dark World | 75559356 |
| 298 | Wicked Dragon with the Ersatz Head | 02957055 |
| 299 | Sonic Maid | 38942059 |
| 300 | Kurama | 85705804 |
| 301 | Legendary Sword | 61854111 |
| 302 | Sword of Dark Destruction | 37120512 |
| 303 | Dark Energy | 04614116 |
| 304 | Axe of Dispair | 40619825 |
| 305 | Laser Cannon Armor | 77007920 |
| 306 | Insect Armor With A Laser Cannon | 03492538 |
| 307 | Elf's Light | 39897277 |
| 308 | Beast Fangs | 46009906 |
| 309 | Steel Shell | 02370081 |
| 310 | Vile Germs | 39774685 |
| 311 | Black Pendant | 65169794 |
| 312 | Silver Bow and Arrow | 01557499 |
| 313 | Horn of Light | 38552107 |
| 314 | Horn of the Unicorn | 64047146 |
| 315 | Dragon Treasure | 01435851 |
| 316 | Electro-Whip | 37820550 |
| 317 | Cyber Shield | 63224564 |
| 318 | Elegant Egotist | 90219263 |

| Number | Card | Password |
|--------|------|----------|
| 319 | Mystical Moon | 36607978 |
| 320 | Stop Defense | 63102017 |
| 321 | Malevolent Nuzzeler | 99597615 |
| 322 | Violet Crystal | 15052462 |
| 323 | Book of Secret Arts | 91595718 |
| 324 | Invigoration | 98374133 |
| 325 | Machine Conversion Factory | 25769732 |
| 326 | Raise Body Heat | 51267887 |
| 327 | Follow Wind | 98252586 |
| 328 | Power of Kaishin | 77027445 |
| 329 | Dragon Capture Jar | 50045299 |
| 330 | Forest | 87430998 |
| 331 | Wasteland | 23424603 |
| 332 | Mountain | 50913601 |
| 333 | Sogen | 86318356 |
| 334 | Umi | 22702055 |
| 335 | Yami | 59197169 |
| 336 | Dark Hole | 53129443 |
| 337 | Raigeki | 12580477 |
| 338 | Mooyan Curry | 58074572 |
| 339 | Red Medicine | 38199696 |
| 340 | Goblin's Secret Remedy | 11868825 |
| 341 | Soul of the Pure | 47852924 |
| 342 | Dian Keto the Cure Master | 84257639 |
| 343 | Sparks | 76103675 |
| 344 | Hinotama | 46130346 |
| 345 | Final Flame | 73134081 |
| 346 | Ookazi | 19523799 |
| 347 | Tremendose Fire | 46918794 |
| 348 | Swords of Revealing Light | 72302403 |
| 349 | Spellbinding Circle | 18807108 |
| 350 | Dark Piercing Light | 45895206 |
| 351 | Yaranzo | 71280811 |
| 352 | Kanan the Swordmistress | 12829151 |
| 353 | Takriminos | 44073668 |
| 354 | Stuffed Animal | 71068263 |
| 355 | Megasonic Eye | 07562372 |
| 356 | Super War-Lion | 33951077 |
| 357 | Yamadron | 70345785 |
| 358 | Seiyaryu | 06740720 |
| 359 | Three-legged Zombie | 33734439 |
| 360 | Zera the Mant | 69123138 |
| 361 | Flying Penguin | 05628232 |

| Number | Card | Password |
|--------|------|----------|
| 362 | Millennium Shield | 32012841 |
| 363 | Fairy's Gift | 68401546 |
| 364 | Black Luster Soldier | 05405694 |
| 365 | Fiend's Mirror | 31890399 |
| 366 | Labyrinth Wall | 67284908 |
| 367 | Jirai Gumo | 94773007 |
| 368 | Shadow Ghoul | 30778711 |
| 369 | Wall Shadow | 63182310 |
| 370 | Labyrinth Tank | 99551425 |
| 371 | Sanga of the Thunder | 25955164 |
| 372 | Kazejin | 62340868 |
| 373 | Suijin | 98434877 |
| 374 | Gate Guardian | 25833572 |
| 375 | Dungeon Worm | 51228280 |
| 376 | Monster Tamer | 97612389 |
| 377 | Ryu-Kishin Powered | 24611934 |
| 378 | Swordstalker | 50005633 |
| 379 | La Jinn the Mystical Genie | 97590747 |
| 380 | Blue Eyes Ultimate Dragon | 23995346 |
| 381 | Toon Alligator | 59383041 |
| 382 | Rude Kaiser | 26378150 |
| 383 | Parrot Dragon | 62762898 |
| 384 | Dark Rabbit | 99261403 |
| 385 | Bickuribox | 25655502 |
| 386 | Harpie's Pet Dragon | 52040216 |
| 387 | Mystic Lamp | 98049915 |
| 388 | Pendulum Machine | 24433920 |
| 389 | Giltia the D. Knight | 51828629 |
| 390 | Launcher Spider | 87322377 |
| 391 | Zoa | 24311372 |
| 392 | Metalzoa | 50705071 |
| 393 | Zone Eater | 86100785 |
| 394 | Steel Scorpion | 13599884 |
| 395 | Dancing Elf | 59983499 |
| 396 | Ocubeam | 86088138 |
| 397 | Leghul | 12472242 |
| 398 | Ooguchi | 58861941 |
| 399 | Swordsman from the Foreign Land | 85255550 |
| 400 | Emperor of the Land and Sea | 11250655 |
| 401 | Ushi Oni | 48649353 |
| 402 | Monster Eye | 84133008 |
| 403 | Leogun | 10538007 |
| 404 | Tatsunootoshigo | 47922711 |

| Number | Card | Password |
|--------|------|----------|
| 405 | Saber Slasher | 73911410 |
| 406 | Yaiba Robo | 10315429 |
| 407 | Machine King | 46700124 |
| 408 | Giant Mech-Soldier | 72299832 |
| 409 | Metal Dragon | 09293977 |
| 410 | Mechanical Spider | 45688586 |
| 411 | Bat | 72076281 |
| 412 | Giga-Tech Wolf | 08471389 |
| 413 | Cyber Soldier | 44865098 |
| 414 | Shovel Crusher | 71950093 |
| 415 | Mechanicalchacer | 07359741 |
| 416 | Blocker | 34743446 |
| 417 | Blast Juggler | 70138455 |
| 418 | Golgoil | 07526150 |
| 419 | Giganto | 33621868 |
| 420 | Cyber-Stein | 69015963 |
| 421 | Cyber Commander | 06400512 |
| 422 | Jinzo #7 | 32809211 |
| 423 | Dice Armadillo | 69893315 |
| 424 | Sky Dragon | 95288024 |
| 425 | Thunder Dragon | 31786629 |
| 426 | Stone D. | 68171737 |
| 427 | Kaiser Dragon | 94566432 |
| 428 | Magician of Faith | 31560081 |
| 429 | Goddess of Whim | 67959180 |
| 430 | Water Magician | 93343894 |
| 431 | Ice Water | 20848593 |
| 432 | Waterdragon Fairy | 66836598 |
| 433 | Ancient Elf | 93221206 |
| 434 | Beautiful Beast Trainer | 29616941 |
| 435 | Water Girl | 55014050 |
| 436 | White Dolphin | 92409659 |
| 437 | Deepsea Shark | 28593363 |
| 438 | Metal Fish | 55998462 |
| 439 | Bottom Dweller | 81386177 |
| 440 | 7 Colored Fish | 23771716 |
| 441 | Mech Bass | 50176820 |
| 442 | Aqua Dragon | 86164529 |
| 443 | Sea King Dragon | 23659124 |
| 444 | Turu-Purun | 59053232 |
| 445 | Guardian of the Sea | 85448931 |
| 446 | Aqua Snake | 12436646 |
| 447 | Giant Red Snake | 58831685 |
| 448 | Spike Seadra | 85326399 |

| Number | Card | Password |
|--------|------|----------|
| 449 | 30,000-Year White Turtle | 11714098 |
| 450 | Kappa Avenger | 48109103 |
| 451 | Kanikabuto | 84103702 |
| 452 | Zarigun | 10598400 |
| 453 | Millennium Golem | 47986555 |
| 454 | Destroyer Golem | 73481154 |
| 455 | Barrel Rock | 10476868 |
| 456 | Minomushi Warrior | 46864967 |
| 457 | Stone Ghost | 72269672 |
| 458 | Kaminari Attack | 09653271 |
| 459 | Tripwire Beast | 45042329 |
| 460 | Bolt Escargot | 12146024 |
| 461 | Bolt Penguin | 48531733 |
| 462 | The Immortal of Thunder | 84926738 |
| 463 | Electric Snake | 11324436 |
| 464 | Wing Eagle | 47319141 |
| 465 | Punished Eagle | 74703140 |
| 466 | Skull Red Bird | 10202894 |
| 467 | Crimson Sunbird | 46696593 |
| 468 | Queen Bird | 73081602 |
| 469 | Armed Ninja | 09076207 |
| 470 | Magical Ghost | 46474915 |
| 471 | Soul Hunter | 72869010 |
| 472 | Air Eater | 08353769 |
| 473 | Vermillion Sparrow | 35752363 |
| 474 | Sea Kamen | 71746462 |
| 475 | Sinister Serpent | 08131171 |
| 476 | Ganigumo | 34536276 |
| 477 | Aliensection | 70924884 |
| 478 | Insect Soldiers of the Sky | 07019529 |
| 479 | Cockroach Knight | 33413638 |
| 480 | Kuwagata Alpha | 60802233 |
| 481 | Burglar | 06297941 |
| 482 | Pragtical | 33691040 |
| 483 | Garvas | 69780745 |
| 484 | Amoeba | 95174353 |
| 485 | Korogashi | 32569498 |
| 486 | Boo Koo | 68963107 |
| 487 | Flower Wolf | 95952802 |
| 488 | Rainbow Flower | 21347810 |
| 489 | Barrel Lily | 67841515 |
| 490 | Needle Ball | 94230224 |
| 491 | Peacock | 20624263 |

| Number | Card | Password |
|--------|------|----------|
| 492 | Hoshinigen | 67629977 |
| 493 | Maha Vailo | 93013676 |
| 494 | Rainbow Marine Mermaid | 29402771 |
| 495 | Musicain King | 56907389 |
| 496 | Wilmee | 92391084 |
| 497 | Yado Karu | 29380133 |
| 498 | Morinphen | 55784832 |
| 499 | Kattapillar | 81179446 |
| 500 | Dragon Seeker | 28563545 |
| 501 | Man-Eater Bug | 54652250 |
| 502 | D. Human | 81057959 |
| 503 | Turtle Raccoon | 17441953 |
| 504 | Fungi of the Musk | 53830602 |
| 505 | Prisman | 80234301 |
| 506 | Gale Dogra | 16229315 |
| 507 | Crazy Fish | 53713014 |
| 508 | Cyber Saurus | 89112729 |
| 509 | Bracchio-Raidus | 16507828 |
| 510 | Laughing Flower | 42591472 |
| 511 | Bean Soldier | 84990171 |
| 512 | Cannon Soldier | 11384280 |
| 513 | Guardian of the Throne Room | 47879985 |
| 514 | Brave Scizzar | 74277583 |
| 515 | The Statue of Easter Island | 10262698 |
| 516 | Muka Muka | 46657337 |
| 517 | Sand Stone | 73051941 |
| 518 | Boulder Tortoise | 09540040 |
| 519 | Fire Kraken | 46534755 |
| 520 | Turtle Bird | 72929454 |
| 521 | Skullbird | 08327462 |
| 522 | Monstrous Bird | 35712107 |
| 523 | The Bistro Butcher | 71107816 |
| 524 | Star Boy | 08201910 |
| 525 | Spirit of the Mountain | 34690519 |
| 526 | Neck Hunter | 70084224 |
| 527 | Milus Radiant | 07489323 |
| 528 | Togex | 33878931 |
| 529 | Flame Cerberus | 60862676 |
| 530 | Eldeen | 06367785 |
| 531 | Mystical Sand | 32751480 |
| 532 | Gemini Elf | 69140098 |
| 533 | Kwagar Hercules | 95144193 |
| 534 | Minar | 32539892 |

| Number | Card | Password |
|--------|------|----------|
| 535 | Kamakiriman | 68928540 |
| 536 | Mechaleon | 94412545 |
| 537 | Mega Thunderball | 21817254 |
| 538 | Niwatori | 07805359 |
| 539 | Corroding Shark | 34290067 |
| 540 | Skelengel | 60694662 |
| 541 | Hanehane | 07089711 |
| 542 | Misairuzame | 33178416 |
| 543 | Tongyo | 69572024 |
| 544 | Dharma Cannon | 96967123 |
| 545 | Skelgon | 32355828 |
| 546 | Wow Warrior | 69750536 |
| 547 | Griggle | 95744531 |
| 548 | Bone Mouse | 21239280 |
| 549 | Frog the Jam | 68638985 |
| 550 | Behegon | 94022093 |
| 551 | Dark Elf | 21417692 |
| 552 | Winged Dragon #2 | 57405307 |
| 553 | Mushroom Man #2 | 93900406 |
| 554 | Lava Battleguard | 20394040 |
| 555 | Tyhone #2 | 56789759 |
| 556 | The Wandering Doomed | 93788854 |
| 557 | Steel Ogre Grotto #1 | 29172562 |
| 558 | Pot the Trick | 55567161 |
| 559 | Oscillo Hero | 82065276 |
| 560 | Invader from Another Planet | 28450915 |
| 561 | Lesser Dragon | 55444629 |
| 562 | Needle Worm | 81843628 |
| 563 | Wretched Ghost of the Attic | 17238333 |
| 564 | Great Mammoth of Goldfine | 54622031 |
| 565 | Man-Eating Black Shark | 80727036 |
| 566 | Yormungarde | 17115745 |
| 567 | Darkworld Thorns | 43500484 |
| 568 | Anthrosaurus | 89904598 |
| 569 | Drooling Lizard | 16353197 |
| 570 | Trakadon | 42348802 |
| 571 | B. Dragon Jungle King | 89832901 |
| 572 | Empress Judge | 15237615 |
| 573 | Little D. | 42625254 |
| 574 | Witch of the Black Forest | 78010363 |
| 575 | Ancient One of the Deep Forest | 14015067 |
| 576 | Giant Scorpion of the Tundra | 41403766 |

| Number | Card | Password |
|--------|------|----------|
| 577 | Crow Goblin | 77998771 |
| 578 | Leo Wizard | 04392470 |
| 579 | Abyss Flower | 40387124 |
| 580 | Patrol Robo | 76775123 |
| 581 | Takuhee | 03170832 |
| 582 | Dark Witch | 35565537 |
| 583 | Weather Report | 72053645 |
| 584 | Binding Chain | 08058240 |
| 585 | Mechanical Snail | 34442949 |
| 586 | Greenkappa | 61831093 |
| 587 | Mon Larvas | 07225792 |
| 588 | Living Vase | 34320307 |
| 589 | Tentacle Plant | 60715406 |
| 590 | Beaked Snake | 06103114 |
| 591 | Morphing Jar | 33508719 |
| 592 | Muse-A | 69992868 |
| 593 | Giant Turtle Who Feeds on Flames | 96981563 |
| 594 | Rose Spectre of Dunn | 32485271 |
| 595 | Fiend Reflection #1 | 68870276 |
| 596 | Ghoul With An Appetite | 95265975 |
| 597 | Pale Beast | 21263083 |
| 598 | Little Chimera | 68658728 |
| 599 | Violent Rain | 94042337 |
| 600 | Key Mace #2 | 20541432 |
| 601 | Tenderness | 57935140 |
| 602 | Penguin Soldier | 93920745 |
| 603 | Fairy Dragon | 20315854 |
| 604 | Obese Marmot of Nefariousness | 56713552 |
| 605 | Liquid Beast | 93108297 |
| 606 | Twin Long Rods #2 | 29692206 |
| 607 | Great Bill | 55691901 |
| 608 | Shining Friendship | 82085619 |
| 609 | Bladefly | 28470714 |
| 610 | Electric Lizard | 55875323 |
| 611 | Hiro's Shadow Scout | 81863068 |
| 612 | Lady of Faith | 17358176 |
| 613 | Twin-headed Thunder Dragon | 54752875 |
| 614 | Hunter Spider | 80141480 |
| 615 | Armored Starfish | 17535588 |
| 616 | Hourglass of Courage | 43530283 |
| 617 | Marine Beast | 29929832 |
| 618 | Warrior of Tradition | 56413937 |
| 619 | Rock Spirit | 82818645 |

| Number | Card | Password |
|--------|------|----------|
| 620 | Snakeyashi | 29802344 |
| 621 | Succubus Knight | 55291359 |
| 622 | Ill Witch | 81686058 |
| 623 | The Thing that Hides in the Mud | 18180762 |
| 624 | High Tide Gyojin | 54579801 |
| 625 | Fairy of the Fountain | 81563416 |
| 626 | Amazon of the Seas | 17968114 |
| 627 | Nekogal #2 | 43352213 |
| 628 | Witch's Apprentice | 80741828 |
| 629 | Armored Rat | 16246527 |
| 630 | Ancient Lizard Warrior | 43230671 |
| 631 | Maiden of the Moonlight | 79629370 |
| 632 | Stone Ogre Grotto | 15023985 |
| 633 | Winged Egg of New Life | 42418084 |
| 634 | Night Lizard | 78402798 |
| 635 | Queen's Double | 05901497 |
| 636 | Blue Winged Crown | 41396436 |
| 637 | Trent | 78780140 |
| 638 | Queen of the Autumn Leaves | 04179849 |
| 639 | Amphibious Bugroth | 40173854 |
| 640 | Acid Crawler | 77568553 |
| 641 | Invader of the Throne | 03056267 |
| 642 | Mystical Sheep #1 | 30451366 |
| 643 | Disk Magician | 76446915 |
| 644 | Flame Viper | 02830619 |
| 645 | Royal Guard | 39239728 |
| 646 | Gruesome Goo | 65623423 |
| 647 | Hyosube | 02118022 |
| 648 | Machine Attacker | 38116136 |
| 649 | Hibikime | 64501875 |
| 650 | Whiptail Crow | 91996584 |
| 651 | Kunai with Chain | 37390589 |
| 652 | Magical Labyrinth | 64389297 |
| 653 | Warrior Elimination | 90873992 |
| 654 | Salamandra | 32268901 |
| 655 | Cursebraker | 69666645 |
| 656 | Eternal Rest | 95051344 |
| 657 | Megamorph | 22046459 |
| 658 | Metalmorph | 68540058 |
| 659 | Winged Trumpeter | 94939166 |
| 660 | Stain Storm | 21323861 |
| 661 | Crush Card | 57728570 |
| 662 | Eradicading Aerosol | 94716515 |

| Number | Card | Password |
|--------|------|----------|
| 663 | Breath of Light | 20101223 |
| 664 | Eternal Drought | 56606928 |
| 665 | Curse of the Millennium Shield | 83094937 |
| 666 | Yamadron Ritual | 29089635 |
| 667 | Gate Guardian Ritual | 56483330 |
| 668 | Bright Castle | 82878489 |
| 669 | Shadow Spell | 29267084 |
| 670 | Black Luster Ritual | 55761792 |
| 671 | Zera Ritual | 81756897 |
| 672 | Harpie's Feather Duster | 18144506 |
| 673 | War-Lion Ritual | 54539105 |
| 674 | Beastry Mirror Ritual | 81933259 |
| 675 | Ultimate Dragon | 17928958 |
| 676 | Commencement Dance | 43417563 |
| 677 | Hamburger Recipe | 80811661 |
| 678 | Revival of Sengenjin | 16206366 |
| 679 | Novox's Prayer | 43694075 |
| 680 | Curse of Tri-Horned Dragon | 79699070 |
| 681 | House of Adhesive Tape | 15083728 |
| 682 | Eatgaboon | 42578427 |
| 683 | Bear Trap | 78977532 |
| 684 | Invisible Wire | 15361130 |
| 685 | Acid Trap Hole | 41356845 |
| 686 | Widespread Ruin | 77754944 |
| 687 | Goblin Fan | 04149689 |
| 688 | Bad Reaction to Simochi | 40633297 |
| 689 | Reverse Trap | 77622396 |
| 690 | Fake Trap | 03027001 |
| 691 | Revival of Serpent Night Dragon | 39411600 |
| 692 | Turtle Oath | 76806714 |
| 693 | Contruct of Mask | 02304453 |
| 694 | Resurrection of Chakra | 39399168 |
| 695 | Puppet Ritual | 05783166 |
| 696 | Javelin Beetle Pact | 41182875 |
| 697 | Garma Sword Oath | 78577570 |
| 698 | Cosmo Queen's Prayer | 04561679 |
| 699 | Revival of Skeleton Rider | 31066283 |
| 700 | Fortress Whale's Oath | 77454922 |
| 701 | Performance of Sword | 04849037 |
| 702 | Hungery Burger | 30243636 |
| 703 | Sengenjin | 76232340 |
| 704 | Skull Guardian | 03627449 |
| 705 | Tri-Horned Dragon | 39111158 |

| Number | Card | Password |
|---|---|---|
| 706 | Serpent Night Dragon | 66516792 |
| 707 | Skull Knight | 02504891 |
| 708 | Cosmo Queen | 38999506 |
| 709 | Charka | 65393205 |
| 710 | Crab Turtle | 91782219 |
| 711 | Mikazukinoyaiba | 38277918 |
| 712 | Meteor Dragon | 64271667 |
| 713 | Meteor B. Dragon | 90660762 |
| 714 | Firewing Pegasus | 27054370 |
| 715 | Psyco Puppet | 63459075 |
| 716 | Garma Sword | 90844184 |
| 717 | Javelin Beetle | 26932788 |
| 718 | Fortress Whale | 62337487 |
| 719 | Dokurorider | 99721536 |
| 720 | Mask of Shine and Dark | 25110231 |
| 721 | Dark | 76792184 |
| 722 | Magician of Black Chaos | 30208479 |

# Games List

ALIENS VS. PREDATOR: EXTINCTION . . . . . . . . . . .109

APEX . . . . . . . . . . . . . . . . . . . . . . . . . . . . . . . . . . .109

BALDUR'S GATE: DARK ALLIANCE . . . . . . . . . . . . .109

BATMAN VENGEANCE . . . . . . . . . . . . . . . . . . . . . .110

BATTLE ENGINE AQUILA . . . . . . . . . . . . . . . . . . . .110

BIG MUTHA TRUCKERS . . . . . . . . . . . . . . . . . . . . . .110

BRUTE FORCE . . . . . . . . . . . . . . . . . . . . . . . . . . . .111

CHASE: HOLLYWOOD STUNT DRIVER . . . . . . . . .112

COLIN MCRAE RALLY 4 . . . . . . . . . . . . . . . . . . . . .112

CONFLICT DESERT STORM . . . . . . . . . . . . . . . . . .113

CRAZY TAXI 3: HIGH ROLLER . . . . . . . . . . . . . . . .113

DAKAR 2: THE WORLD'S ULTIMATE RALLY . . . . . .114

DEATHROW . . . . . . . . . . . . . . . . . . . . . . . . . . . . . .115

DIE HARD: VENDETTA . . . . . . . . . . . . . . . . . . . . . .115

DR. MUTO . . . . . . . . . . . . . . . . . . . . . . . . . . . . . . .115

DUNGEONS AND DRAGONS HEROES . . . . . . . . . .116

ENTER THE MATRIX . . . . . . . . . . . . . . . . . . . . . . . .118

FINDING NEMO . . . . . . . . . . . . . . . . . . . . . . . . . . .118

FREEDOM FIGHTERS . . . . . . . . . . . . . . . . . . . . . . .119

GODZILLA: DESTROY ALL MONSTERS MELEE . . . .120

HITMAN 2: SILENT ASSASSIN . . . . . . . . . . . . . . . .124

HULK . . . . . . . . . . . . . . . . . . . . . . . . . . . . . . . . . . .125

INDIANA JONES AND THE EMPEROR'S TOMB . . . .126

JAMES BOND 007: NIGHTFIRE . . . . . . . . . . . . . . . .126

JURASSIC PARK: OPERATION GENESIS . . . . . . . . .130

KUNG FU CHAOS . . . . . . . . . . . . . . . . . . . . . . . . . .132

MACE GRIFFIN BOUNTY HUNTER . . . . . . . . . . . . .133

MEDAL OF HONOR: FRONTLINE . . . . . . . . . . . . . .134

MINORITY REPORT . . . . . . . . . . . . . . . . . . . . . . . .136

# Xbox™

MIDNIGHT CLUB II . . . . . . . . . . . . . . . . . . . . . . . . . .138

MIDTOWN MADNESS 3 . . . . . . . . . . . . . . . . . . . . .139

MLB SLUGFEST 2004 . . . . . . . . . . . . . . . . . . . . . . .139

NAMCO MUSEUM VOL. I . . . . . . . . . . . . . . . . . . . .142

NASCAR THUNDER 2004 . . . . . . . . . . . . . . . . . . . .145

NBA 2K3 . . . . . . . . . . . . . . . . . . . . . . . . . . . . . . . . . .145

NBA INSIDE DRIVE 2003 . . . . . . . . . . . . . . . . . . . .146

NBA LIVE 2003 . . . . . . . . . . . . . . . . . . . . . . . . . . . .147

NBA STREET VOL. 2 . . . . . . . . . . . . . . . . . . . . . . . .149

NICKELODEON PARTY BLAST . . . . . . . . . . . . . . . .150

OUTLAW VOLLEYBALL . . . . . . . . . . . . . . . . . . . . .150

PHANTOM CRASH . . . . . . . . . . . . . . . . . . . . . . . . .151

PIRATES OF THE CARIBBEAN . . . . . . . . . . . . . . . .151

PRO RACE DRIVER . . . . . . . . . . . . . . . . . . . . . . . . .152

QUANTUM REDSHIFT . . . . . . . . . . . . . . . . . . . . . .152

RED FACTION II . . . . . . . . . . . . . . . . . . . . . . . . . . .152

ROCKY . . . . . . . . . . . . . . . . . . . . . . . . . . . . . . . . . . .153

ROLLER COASTER TYCOON . . . . . . . . . . . . . . . . .155

RUN LIKE HELL . . . . . . . . . . . . . . . . . . . . . . . . . . .155

SCOOBY-DOO: NIGHT OF 100 FRIGHTS . . . . . . .156

SERIOUS SAM . . . . . . . . . . . . . . . . . . . . . . . . . . . . .157

SPEED KINGS . . . . . . . . . . . . . . . . . . . . . . . . . . . . .157

SPLINTER CELL . . . . . . . . . . . . . . . . . . . . . . . . . . . .159

STARSKY AND HUTCH . . . . . . . . . . . . . . . . . . . . .159

STAR WARS JEDI KNIGHT II: JEDI OUTCAST . . . . .159

STAR WARS: JEDI STARFIGHTER . . . . . . . . . . . . . .160

STAR WARS: KNIGHTS OF THE OLD REPUBLIC . . .161

STAR WARS: THE CLONE WARS . . . . . . . . . . . . . . .161

STATE OF EMERGENCY . . . . . . . . . . . . . . . . . . . . .162

# Xbox™

STEEL BATTALION ...........................164

SUPERMAN: THE MAN OF STEEL ...............164

THE ELDER SCROLLS: MORROWIND ..........165

THE GREAT ESCAPE ..........................165

THE LORD OF THE RINGS: THE TWO TOWERS ...166

THE SIMPSONS: HIT & RUN ...................167

THE SIMS ...................................168

TIGER WOODS PGA TOUR 2004 ..............169

TOM CLANCY'S GHOST RECON ..............170

TOM CLANCY'S GHOST RECON:
ISLAND THUNDER ...........................171

TONY HAWK'S PRO SKATER 4 ................171

WAKEBOARDING UNLEASHED ................174

X2: WOLVERINE'S REVENGE ...................174

X-MEN: NEXT DIMENSION ....................175

# ALIENS VS. PREDATOR: EXTINCTION

### Cheats

Pause the game during a campaign and press R, R, L, R, L, L, R, L, R, R, L, R, L, L, R, L. You will find the Cheats in the Options menu.

# APEX

### All Tracks and Circuits

Start a new game in Dream mode and enter WORLD as a brand name.

### All Concept Cars

Start a new game in Dream mode and enter DREAMY as a brand name.

### All Production Cars

Start a new game in Dream mode and enter REALITY as a brand name.

# BALDUR'S GATE: DARK ALLIANCE

### All Spells

During gameplay, hold Y + A + L all the way + R halfway, then press the Left Thumbstick right.

### Invincibility and Level Warp

During gameplay, hold Y + A + L all the way + R halfway + Left Thumbstick right, then press START.

# BATMAN VENGEANCE

**Master Code**

At the Main Menu press L, R, L, R, X, X, Y, Y.

**Unlimited Electric Batarangs**

At the Main Menu press L, R, B, White, L.

**Unlimited Batarangs**

At the Main Menu press L, R, White, Y.

# BATTLE ENGINE AQUILA

**Level Select**

Start a new game and enter !EVAH!.

**God Mode**

Start a new game and enter B4K42.

**All Bonuses**

Start a new game and enter I05770Y2.

# BIG MUTHA TRUCKERS

Select Cheats from the Options screen and enter the following:

**All Cheats**
Enter CHEATIN MUTHATRUCKER.

**Level Select**
Enter LAZYPLAYER.

**Unlimited Time**
Enter PUBLICTRANSPORT.

**$10 Million**
Enter LOTSAMONEY.

**Evil Truck**
Enter VARLEY.

**Fast Truck**
Enter GINGERBEER.

**Diplomatic Immunity**
Enter VICTORS.

**Disable Damage**
Enter 6WL.

**Automatic Sat Nav**
Enter USETHEFORCE.

**Small Pedestrians**
Enter DAISHI.

# BRUTE FORCE

Before using the following codes, you need to go through the full ending once and collect all the DNA canisters.

## All Characters

Create a new profile with the name GARNER.

## All Missions

Create a new profile with the name VENGAR.

## Rapid Fire

Create a new profile with the name RAPIDFIRE.

## Stronger

Create a new profile with the name MATTSOELL.

## Tougher Game

Create a new profile with the name BRUTAL.

## Dumb Enemy AI

Create a new profile with the name SPRAGNT.

## Better Aim

Create a new profile with the name DEADAIM.

## Better Defense

Create a new profile with the name ERINROBERTS.

## Easier Kills and Deaths

Create a new profile with the name DBLDAY.

## Cartoon

Create a new profile with the name HVYMTL.

# CHASE:
# HOLLYWOOD STUNT DRIVER

Select Career Mode and enter the following as the user-name:

**Unlock Everything**
Enter Dare Angel.

**All Cars and Challenges**
Enter Ride On.

**All Cars and Multiplayer Modes**
Enter BAM4FUN.

**Level Select**
Enter Action Star.

# COLIN MCRAE RALLY 4

**Cheat Mode**
Select Secrets from the Options and enter the following:

**Group B with Cars**
Enter CFCKGL.

**All Other Cars**
Enter AIDLAU.

**All Car Parts**
Enter FUDWHC.

**All Tracks**
Enter BSDJUC.

**Mirror Tracks**
Enter EPDZJF.

**All Tests**
Enter DMLPOD.

**All Weather**
Enter CLRWTR.

**Expert Mode**
Enter HIQNRM.

## CONFLICT DESERT STORM

### Cheat Mode

At the Main Menu, press X, X, Y, Y, press Left Analog Stick (x2), Right Analog Stick (x2), press L, L, R, R. Pause the game to find the Cheats in the Options screen.

## CRAZY TAXI 3: HIGH ROLLER

### No Destination Mark and Arrow

At the Character Select screen, hold White + Black and press A. The word "Expert" appears at the bottom of the screen when entered correctly.

### No Arrows

At the Character Select screen, hold White and press A. The message "no arrows" appears at the bottom of the screen when entered correctly.

**No Destination Mark**

At the Character Select screen, hold Black and press A. The message "no destination mark" appears at the bottom of the screen when entered correctly.

# DAKAR 2: THE WORLD'S ULTIMATE RALLY

Select Cheat Code from the Extras menu and enter the following:

**All Vehicles**
Enter SWEETAS

**All Tracks**
Enter BONZER

# DEATHROW

**Unlock Everything**

Enter the name SOUTHEND.

**All Teams and Players**

Name Player 4 ALL150.

**All Arenas**

Name Player 4 MORE ROOM.

**Extreme Difficulty**

Name Player 4 NO FEAR.

**Multidisc**

Name Player 4 CONFUSED.

# DIE HARD: VENDETTA

Enter the following codes at the Main Menu. A message appears when the code is correctly entered.

**Invulnerable**

Press L, R, L, R, L, R, L, R.

**Unlimited Ammunition**

Press White(x4), L, R.

**All Levels**

Press X, Y, White, White, X, Y, White, White.

**Flame On**

Press X, Y, B, X, Y, B.

**Infinite Hero Time**

Press B, X, Y, White, R, L.

**Liquid Metal**

Press B, Y, X, B, Y, X.

**Big Heads**

Press R(x2), L, R.

**Pin Heads**

Press L(x2), R, L.

**Exploding Fists**

Press B, X, R(x2).

**Hot Fists**

Press X, B, Y, L(x2).

**Exploding Bullets**

Press L, R, White, Y, B.

**I Got The Power Mode**

Press White, B, White, B, White, B.

# DR. MUTO

Select Cheats from the Options screen to enter the following:

**Invincibility**
Enter NECROSCI. This doesn't work when falling from high above.

**Never Take Damage**
Enter CHEATERBOY.

**Unlock Every Gadget**
Enter TINKERTOY.

**Unlock Every Morph**
Enter EUREKA.

**Go Anywhere**
Enter BEAMMEUP.

**Secret Morphs**
Enter LOGGLOGG.

**See the Movies**
Enter HOTTICKET.

**Super Ending**
Enter BUZZOFF.

# DUNGEONS AND DRAGONS HEROES

During a game, hold L and press A + Y. Now you can enter the following:

**Invincibility**
Enter PELOR.

**Nightmare Difficulty Setting**
Enter MPS LABS.

**Unlimited Mystical Will**
Enter OBADHAI.

**10,000 Experience Points**
Enter DSP633.

**500,000 Gold**
Enter KNE637.

**Dexterity Up 10**
Enter YAN or ZXE053.

**Constitution Up 10**
Enter N STINE.

**10 Anti-Venom**
Enter SPINRAD.

**10 Berserk Brew**
Enter THOMAS.

**10 Fash Freeze**
Enter ESKO.

**10 Fire Bomb**
Enter WEBER.

**10 Fire Flask**
Enter BROPHY.

**10 Firey Oil**
Enter EHOFF.

**10 Globe Potion**
Enter WRIGHT.

**10 Insect Plague**
Enter DERISO.

**10 Keys**
Enter KEIDEL.

**10 Keys**
Enter SNODGRASS.

**10 Large Healing Potions**
Enter THOMPSON.

## Xbox™     D

**10 Large Will Potions**
Enter GEE.

**10 Medium Potions of Will**
Enter LU.

**10 Potions of Haste**
Enter UHL.

**10 Pyrokins**
Enter SMITH.

**10 Rod of Destruction**
Enter AUSTIN.

**10 Rod of Fire**
Enter DELUCIA.

**10 Rod of Miracles**
Enter JARMAN.

**10 Rod of Missiles**
Enter MILLER.

**10 Rod of Reflection**
Enter WHITTAKE.

**10 Rod of Shadows**
Enter DINOLT.

**10 Thrown Axe of Ruin**
Enter RAMERO.

**10 Thrown Daggers of Stunning**
Enter BELL.

**10 Thrown Daggers**
Enter MOREL.

**10 Thrown Halcyon Hammers**
Enter PRASAD.

**10 Thrown Hammer**
Enter BRATHWAI.

**10 Thrown Viper Axe**
Enter FRAZIER.

**10 Thrown Viper Axe**
Enter HOWARD.

**10 Thuderstone**
Enter ELSON.

**10 Tome of Lessons**
Enter PAQUIN.

**10 Tome of the Apprentice**
Enter BILGER.

**10 Tome of the Teacher**
Enter MEFFORD.

**10 Tomes of the Master**
Enter SPANBURG.

**10 Warp Stones**
Enter HOPPENST.

**10 Holy Water**
Enter CRAWLEY.

**View Concept Art**
Enter CONCEPTS.

**View Credits**
Enter CREDITS.

**Disable Cheats**
Enter UNBUFF.

# ENTER THE MATRIX

### Cheat Mode

After playing through the hacking system and unlocking CHEAT.EXE, use CHEAT.EXE to enter the following:

| Effect | Code |
| --- | --- |
| All Guns | 0034AFFF |
| Infinite Ammo | 1DDF2556 |
| Invisibility | FFFFFFF1 |
| Infinite Focus | 69E5D9E4 |
| Infinite Health | 7F4DF451 |
| Speedy Logos | 7867F443 |
| Unlock Secret Level | 13D2C77F |
| Fast Focus Restore | FFF0020A |
| Test Level | 13D2C77F |
| Enemies Can't Hear You | 4516DF45 |
| Turbo Mode | FF00001A |
| Multiplayer Fight | D5C55D1E |
| Low Gravity | BB013FFF |
| Taxi Driving | 312MF451 |

# FINDING NEMO

Enter the following at the main menu. The word Cheat! will appear if entered correctly. Pause the game at the level select to access the cheats.

### Level Select

Press Y (x3), X, X, B, X, Y, B, X, Y, X, Y, X, Y, B, Y, Y.

### Invincibility

Press Y, X, X, B (x3), Y, Y, X (x3), B (x4), X, Y, B (x3), X, B, Y, B, B, X, B, B, Y, B, X, B (x3), Y.

### Secret Level

Press Y, X, B, B, X, Y, Y, X, B, B, X, Y, Y, B, X, Y, X, B, B, X, Y.

### Credits

Press Y, X, B, Y, Y, X, B, Y, X, B, Y, X, X, B, Y, X, B, Y, X, B, B, Y, X, B.

# FREEDOM FIGHTERS

### Cheat List

During the game, enter the following:

| | |
|---|---|
| Invisibility | Y, A, X, B, B, Left |
| Infinite ammo | Y, A, X, B, A, Right |
| Max charisma | Y, A, X, B, A, Down |
| Heavy machine gun | Y, A, X, B, Y, Down |
| Nail gun | Y, A, X, B, A, Left |
| Rocket launcher | Y, A, X, B, Y, Left |
| Shotgun | Y, A, X, B, B, Up |
| Sniper rifle | Y, A, X, B, Y, Right |
| Sub machine gun | Y, A, X, B, Y, Up |
| Ragdolls | Y, A, X, B, X, Up |
| Slow motion | Y, A, X, B, B, Right |
| Fast motion | Y, A, X, B, B, Down |
| Change spawn point | Y, A, X, B, A, Up |

# GODZILLA: DESTROY ALL MONSTERS MELEE

At the Main Menu, press and hold L, B, R, then release B, R, L (*in that order*). Enter the following codes:

| Effect | Code |
| --- | --- |
| Twelve Continues in Adventure | 548319 |
| All Gallery | 962129 |

| | |
| --- | --- |
| All Cities and Monsters | 863768 |
| All Monsters, Except Orga | 753079 |
| All Monsters | 209697 |

| Effect | Code |
|---|---|
| Godzilla 2000 | 637522 |
| Rodan | 724284 |
| Destoroyah | 352117 |
| Gigan | 822777 |
| King Ghidorah | 939376 |
| Mecha-Ghidorah | 504330 |
| Mecha Godzilla 2 | 643861 |
| Orga | 622600 |

| | |
|---|---|
| All Cities | 107504 |

| | |
|---|---|
| Monster Island Level | 745749 |
| Mothership Level | 972094 |
| Boxing Ring Level | 440499 |

| Effect | Code |
| --- | --- |
| Military | 728629 |
| Energy Doesn't Recharge, More Damage | 690242 |
| Player Indicators Visible | 860068 |
| No HUD | 880460 |
| Hedorah | 288730 |
| No Hedorah | 584408 |
| Add AI player to Melee | 154974 |
| P1 is Small | 558277 |
| P2 is Small | 689490 |
| P3 is Small | 203783 |
| P4 is Small | 495355 |
| Even Players Are Small | 600095 |
| Odd Players Are Small | 853955 |
| All Players Are Small | 154974 |

| | |
| --- | --- |
| Player Regenerates Health | 597378 |
| P1 Invincible | 152446 |
| P2 Invincible | 724689 |
| P3 Invincible | 367744 |
| P4 Invincible | 317320 |
| All Invincible | 569428 |
| P1 Deals 4x Damage | 940478 |
| P2 Deals 4x Damage | 930041 |
| P3 Deals 4x Damage | 537651 |
| P4 Deals 4x Damage | 889610 |
| All Deal 4x Damage | 817683 |
| Military Deals 4x Damage | 970432 |
| Throw All Buildings and Objects | 248165 |
| Indestructible Buildings | 451129 |

| Effect | Code |
| --- | --- |
| P1 Invisible | 659672 |
| P2 Invisible | 493946 |
| All Monsters Invisible | 600225 |
| P1 Full Energy | 778393 |
| P2 Full Energy | 881557 |
| P3 Full Energy | 597558 |
| P4 Full Energy | 218967 |
| No Freeze Tanks | 223501 |
| No Power-ups | 229497 |
| No Health Power-ups | 221086 |
| No Energy Power-ups | 803358 |
| No Mothra Power-ups | 491040 |
| No Rage Power-ups | 666500 |
| Only Energy Power-ups | 553945 |
| Only Rage Power-ups | 660398 |
| Only Health Power-Ups | 270426 |
| P1 Always in Rage | 159120 |
| P2 Always in Rage | 491089 |
| P3 Always in Rage | 450514 |
| P4 Always in Rage | 702905 |
| Black-and-White | 860475 |
| Technicolor | 394804 |
| Game Version (in options) | 097401 |

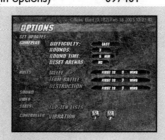

| Effect | Code |
|---|---|
| Credits | 339223 |

## HITMAN 2: SILENT ASSASSIN

### Level Select

At the Main Menu, press R, L, Up, Down, Y, B.

### Complete Level

During gameplay, press R, L, Up, Down, A, X, press Left Analog Stick, B, A, B, A.

### All Weapons

During gameplay, press R, L, Up, Down, A, Up, X, A.

### Invincibilty

During gameplay, press R, L, Up, Down, A, R, L, Black, White.

### Full Heal

During gameplay, press R, L, Up, Down, A, Up, Down.

### Toggle Lethal Charge

During gameplay, press L, R, Up, Down, A, Black, Black.

### Gravity

During gameplay, press R, L, Up, Down, A, L, L.

### Slow Motion

During gameplay, press R, L, Up, Down, A, Up, L.

### Megaforce

During gameplay, press R, L, Up, Down, A, R, R.

**Toggle Bomb Mode**

During gameplay, press R, L, Up, Down, A, Up, White.

**Toggle Punch Mode**

During gameplay, press R, L, Up, Down, A, Up, Up.

**Toggle Nailgun Mode**

During gameplay, press R, L, Up, Down A, White, White.

# HULK

## Cheat Codes

Select Code Input from the Options and enter the following and press Accept. Turn on the cheats by selecting Cheats from the Special Features menu.

| Description | Code Input |
| --- | --- |
| Invulnerability | GMMSKIN |
| Regenerator | FLSHWND |
| Unlimited Continues | GRNCHTR |
| Double Hulk HP | HLTHDSE |
| Double Enemies HP | BRNGITN |
| Half Enemies HP | MMMYHLP |
| Reset High Score | NMBTHIH |
| Full Rage Meter | ANGMNGT |
| Puzzle Solved | BRCESTN |
| Wicked Punch | FSTOFRY |
| Unlock All Levels | TRUBLVR |

## Universal Unlock Codes

Enter the following at the special terminals, called "Universal Code Input," that are found throughout the levels. You will find these bonus materials in the Special Features menu.

| | |
| --- | --- |
| Play as Gray Hulk | JANITOR |
| Desert Battle Art | FIFTEEN |
| Hulk Movie FMV Art | NANOMED |
| Hulk Transformed ART | SANFRAN |
| Hulk vs. Hulk Dogs Art | PITBULL |

# INDIANA JONES AND THE EMPEROR'S TOMB

### Invincible with Unlimited Ammo

At the title screen, hold L + R and press Up, Up, Down, Up, A, X, A, B, Up, Down, Y, Start.

# JAMES BOND 007: NIGHTFIRE

Select Codenames from the Main Menu and choose a codename. Then pick Secret Unlocks to enter the following codes. Save your codename before exiting this menu.

### Level Select

Enter PASSPORT.

### Alpine Escape Level

Enter POWDER.

### Enemies Vanquished Level

Enter TRACTION.

### Double Cross Level

Enter BONSAI.

**Night Shift Level**
Enter HIGHRISE.

**Chain Reaction Level**
Enter MELTDOWN.

**Phoenix Fire Level**
Enter FLAME.

**Deep Descent Level**
Enter AQUA.

**Island Infiltration Level**
Enter PARADISE.

**Countdown Level**
Enter BLASTOFF.

**Equinox Level**
Enter VACUUM.

**All Gadget Upgrades**
Enter Q LAB.

**Camera Upgrade**
Enter SHUTTER.

**Decrypter Upgrade**
Enter SESAME.

**Grapple Upgrade**
Enter LIFTOFF.

**Laser Upgrade**
Enter PHOTON.

**Scope Upgrade**
Enter SCOPE.

**Stunner Upgrade**
Enter ZAP.

**Tranquilizer Dart Upgrade**
Enter SLEEPY.

**Bigger Clip for Sniper Rifle**
Enter MAGAZINE.

**P2K Upgrade**
Enter P2000.

**Golden Wolfram P2K**
Enter AU P2K.

**Golden PP7**
Enter AU PP7.

**Vanquish Car Missile Upgrade**
Enter LAUNCH.

**All Multiplayer Scenarios**
Enter GAMEROOM.

**Uplink Multiplayer Scenario**
Enter TRANSMIT.

**Demolition Multiplayer Scenario**
Enter TNT.

**Protection Multiplayer Scenario**
Enter GUARDIAN.

**GoldenEye Strike Multiplayer Scenario**
Enter ORBIT.

**Assassination Multiplayer Scenario**
Enter TARGET.

**Team King of the Hill Multiplayer Scenario**
Enter TEAMWORK.

**Explosive Scenery Option, Multiplayer**
Enter BOOM. Find this option in the Enviro-Mods menu.

**All Characters, Multiplayer**
Enter PARTY.

**Play as Bond Tux, Multiplayer**
Enter BLACKTIE.

**Play as Drake Suit, Multiplayer**
Enter NUMBER 1.

**Play as Bond Spacesuit, Multiplayer**
Enter ZERO G.

**Play as Goldfinger, Multiplayer**
Enter MIDAS.

**Play as Renard, Multiplayer**
Enter HEADCASE.

**Play as Scaramanga, Multiplayer**
Enter ASSASSIN.

**Play as Christmas Jones, Multiplayer**

Enter NUCLEAR.

**Play as Wai Lin, Multiplayer**

Enter MARTIAL.

**Play as Xenia Onatopp, Multiplayer**

Enter JANUS.

**Play as May Day, Multiplayer**

Enter BADGIRL.

**Play as Elektra King, Multiplayer**

Enter SLICK.

**Play as Jaws, Multiplayer**

Enter DENTAL.

**Play as Baron Samedi, Multiplayer**

Enter VOODOO.

**Play as Oddjob, Multiplayer**

Enter BOWLER.

**Play as Nick Nack, Multiplayer**

Enter BITESIZE.

**Play as Max Zorin, Multiplayer**

Enter BLIMP.

**Drive an SUV, Enemies Vanquished Level**

Start the Enemies Vanquished Level and pause the game. Hold L and press X, B, Y, X, Y, then release L.

**Race the Cobra, Enemies Vanquished Level**

Start the Enemies Vanquished Level and pause the game. Hold L and press B, B, X, X, Y, then release L.

Enter the following codes during the Paris Prelude, Enemies Vanquished, Island Infiltration, or Deep Descent levels:

### Faster Racing

Pause the game, hold L and press X, Y, B, Y, X, then release L.

### Berserk Racing

Pause the game, hold L and press X, Y, Y, X, Y, B, then release L.

### Trails

Pause the game, hold L and press X, B, B, X, then release L.

### Double Armor

Pause the game, hold L and press B, Y, X, B, B, then release L.

### Triple Armor

Pause the game, hold L and press B, Y, X, B, B, B, then release L.

### Quadruple Armor

Pause the game, hold L and press B, Y, X, B (x4), then release L.

### Super Bullets

Pause the game, hold L and press B (x4), release L.

# JURASSIC PARK: OPERATION GENESIS

### Gimme Some Money

During gameplay, press L + Up, L + Down, L + Up. This gives you $10,000.

### Gimme Lots of Money

During gameplay, press L, Right, Right, L, R, Down. This gives you $250,000.

### Where's the Money?

During gameplay, press L, R, L, R, Down, Down. This takes away all your money.

### Impossible Mission

During gameplay, press R, Right (x4), R. This completes all of the missions.

### All Research

During gameplay, press Down (x3), Left, Right, L, Down, Up.

### Mr. DNA

During gameplay, press R, Up, R, Right, L, Down.

### Rampage Time

During gameplay, press L, L, L, Left, Left, Left. This makes all carnivores rampage.

### Extinction Event

During gameplay, press L, R, Down, R, L. This kills all dinosaurs.

### Oh No!

During gameplay, press Left, Right, Left, Right, R. This kills all visitors.

### Dial-A-Twister

During gameplay, press Left, Up, Right, Down, L + R.

### No Twisters

During gameplay, press Left, Right, L, R, Left, Right, L, R.

### Hot One

During gameplay, press R + Down, R + Down. This causes a heat wave.

### Welcome to Melbourne

During gameplay, press R, R, L, R, Down, Up, Down. This causes it to rain.

### Guaranteed Immunity

During gameplay, hold L + R and press Up, Up. Dinosaurs won't get sick.

### No Red Tape

During gameplay, press L, R, Left, Down (x4). You aren't charged for deaths.

### Open to the Public

During gameplay, press Left, Down, Right, Up, L + R, L + R. This gives you the selection of dig sites without the required stars.

### Market Day

During gameplay, press Down, L, R, Down.

### Sequencing Error

During gameplay, press Down, Up + R, L, Down. This gives 55% dinosaur genomes.

### Drive-by

During gameplay, press R + L, Left, Down, Right, Right. The safari ride camera acts like a gun.

### Crash!

During gameplay, hold R + L and press Up, Down, Up, Down.

### Isla Muerta

During gameplay, press R, R, R, L, Right. Dinosaurs appear decayed.

# KUNG FU CHAOS

At the main menu, press the Left Thumbstick and enter the following:

### Master Code

Press Left, Up, X, Up, Right, Y, Left, A, Right, Down.

### Level Select

Press Left, A, Down, Y, Right, A, Down, A, Right.

### All Characters

Press B, A, White, Down, Y, B, A, Left, Left, A, Down.

### All Costumes

Press B, A, Down, B, A, B, Y.

### Character Bios

Press B, Left, A, Right, B, Down, Right, A, White, Left.

### Candi Roll

Press Left, A, Down, Y, Start, Down, A, Y.

### Captain Won Ton

Press Left, A, Right, Down, Y, B, Up, Down.

### Shao Ting

Press White, A, Left, Right, Up, Start, B, A, Left, Down, Y.

**All Ending Movies**

Press B, A, Y, Start, A, White, A, Y.

**Miniseries Mode**

Press Start, Left, Y, Start, Up, B, Up, Right, B.

**Championship Mode**

Press Start, Left, A, Y, Down, A, Y.

**Four Star Bonuses**

Press A, Left, Left, B, Right, A, White, Left.

# MACE GRIFFIN BOUNTY HUNTER

During a game, select the Electro-Cosh and quickly press the following button sequences. A message will confirm a correct code.

**Invincibility**

Press L, R, L, R, A, B, B, A, X, Y.

**Level Skip**

Press L, R, L, R, A, A, B, B, X, B.

**Level Select**

Press L, R, L, R, A, A, B, B, X, X.

**Unlimited Ammo**

Press L, R, L, R, A, B, B, A, X, X.

**Auto Focus**

Press L, R, L, R, A, B, B, A, B, A.

**One Hit Kills**

Press L, R, L, R, A, B, B, A (x3).

**Double Damage**

Press L, R, L, R, A, B, B, A, Y, Y.

**Big Heads**

Press L, R, L, R, A, B, B, A, B, B.

**Detach Camera**

Press L, R, L, R, A, B, B, A, Y, X.

# MEDAL OF HONOR: FRONTLINE

Select Passwords from the Options menu and enter the following codes. You need to turn on many of these cheats at the Bonus screen.

## Master Code
Enter ENCHILADA.

## Mission Complete with Gold Star
Enter SALMON.

## Mission 2: A Storm in the Port
Enter BASS.

## Mission 3: Needle in a Haystack
Enter STURGEON.

## Mission 4: Several Bridges Too Far
Enter PIKE.

## Mission 5: Rolling Thunder
Enter TROUT.

## Mission 6: The Horten's Nest
Enter CATFISH.

## Silver Bullet Mode
Enter KILLSHOT.

**Perfectionist**
Enter ONESHOTGUN.

**Achilles' Head**
Enter CRANIUM.

**Bullet Shield**
Enter NOHITSFORU.

**Snipe-O-Rama**
Enter LONGVIEW.

**Rubber Grenade**
Enter FLUBBER.

**Mohton Torpedoes**
Enter TOPFUN.

**Invisible Enemies**
Enter GHOSTARMY.

**Men with Hats**
Enter BOOTDAHEAD.

**A Good Day to "Dye" Video**
Enter COTOBREATH.

**From the Animator's Desk Video**
Enter FLIPBOOK.

**Making of D-Day FMV**
Enter BACKSTAGEO.

**Making of Storm in the Port FMV**
Enter BACKSTAGET.

**Making of Needle in a Hay Stack FMV**
Enter BACKSTAGER.

**Making of Several Bridges Too Far FMV**
Enter BACKSTAGEF.

**Making of Rolling Thunder FMV**
Enter BACKSTAGEI.

**Making of the Horten's Nest FMV**
Enter BACKSTAGES.

# MINORITY REPORT

Select Cheats from the Special menu and enter the following:

**Invincibility**
  Enter LRGARMS.

**Level Warp All**
  Enter PASSKEY.

**Level Skip**
  Enter QUITER.

**All Combos**
  Enter NINJA.

**All Weapons**
  Enter STRAPPED.

**Infinite Ammo**
  Enter MRJUAREZ.

**Super Damage**
  Enter SPINACH.

**Health**
  Enter BUTTERUP.

  Select Alternate Heroes from the Special menu to find the following cheats:

**Clown Hero**
  Enter SCARYCLOWN.

**Convict Hero**
  Enter JAILBREAK.

**GI John Hero**
Enter GNRLINFANTRY.

**Lizard Hero**
Enter HISSSS.

**Moseley Hero**
Enter HAIRLOSS.

**Nara Hero**
Enter WEIGHTGAIN.

**Nikki Hero**
Enter BIGLIPS.

**Robot Hero**
Enter MRROBOTO.

**Super John Hero**
Enter SUPERJOHN.

**Zombie Hero**
Enter IAMSODEAD.

**Free Aim**
Enter FPSSTYLE.

**Pain Arenas**
Enter MAXIMUMHURT.

**Armor**
Enter STEELUP.

**Baseball Bat**
Enter SLUGGER.

**Rag Doll**
Enter CLUMSY.

**Slo-Mo Button**
Enter SLIZOMIZO.

**Bouncy Men**
Enter BOUNZMEN.

**Wreck the Joint**
Enter CLUTZ.

**Dramatic Finish**
Enter STYLIN.

**Ending**
Enter WIMP.

### Concept Art
Enter SKETCHPAD.

### All Movies
Enter DIRECTOR.

### Do Not Select
Enter DONOTSEL.

# MIDNIGHT CLUB II

Select Cheat Codes from the Options and enter the following:

### All Vehicles
Enter hotwired.

### All Cities in Arcade Mode
Enter theworldismine.

### Weapons
Enter lovenotwar. Press the Left Thumbstick and White to fire.

### All Car Abilities
Enter greasemonkey.

### Unlimited Nitrous in Arcade Mode
Enter zoomzoom4.

### Extra Stat
Enter bigbrother.

### Game Speed
Enter one of the following. 0 is slowest, 9 is fastest.

### Change Difficulty
Enter one of the following. 0 is easiest, 9 is hardest.

| howfastcanitbe0 | howhardcanitbe0 |
| howfastcanitbe1 | howhardcanitbe1 |
| howfastcanitbe2 | howhardcanitbe2 |
| howfastcanitbe3 | howhardcanitbe3 |
| howfastcanitbe4 | howhardcanitbe4 |
| howfastcanitbe5 | howhardcanitbe5 |
| howfastcanitbe6 | howhardcanitbe6 |
| howfastcanitbe7 | howhardcanitbe7 |
| howfastcanitbe8 | howhardcanitbe8 |
| howfastcanitbe9 | howhardcanitbe9 |

# MIDTOWN MADNESS 3

### All Cars

At the car select, hold down the Left Thumbstick and press L, R, L, L, L, R, R, R, L, L, R, R.

# MLB SLUGFEST 2004

### Cheats

At the Match-Up screen, use X, Y and B to enter the following codes, then press the appropriate direction. For example, for "No Contact Mode" (433 Left) press X four times, Y three times, B three times, then press Left.

| Code | Enter |
| --- | --- |
| Cheats Disabled | 111 Down |
| Unlimited Turbo | 444 Down |
| No Fatigue | 343 Up |
| No Contact Mode | 433 Left |
| 16' Softball | 242 Down |
| Rubber Ball | 242 Up |
| Whiffle Bat | 004 Right |
| Blade Bat | 002 Up |

| Bone Bat | 001 Up |
| --- | --- |
| Ice Bat | 003 Up |
| Log Bat | 004 Up |
| Mace Bat | 004 Left |

| Spike Bat | 005 Up |
| --- | --- |
| Big Head | 200 Right |
| Tiny Head | 200 Left |
| Max Batting | 300 Left |
| Max Power | 030 Left |
| Max Speed | 003 Left |
| Alien Team | 231 Down |

| Code | Enter |
| --- | --- |
| Bobble Head Team | 133 Down |

| Casey Team | 233 Down |
| --- | --- |
| Dolphin Team | 102 Down |
| Dwarf Team | 103 Down |
| Eagle Team | 212 Right |
| Evil Clown Team | 211 Down |

| Gladiator Team | 113 Down |
| --- | --- |
| Horse Team | 211 Right |
| Lion Team | 220 Right |
| Little League | 101 Down |
| Minotaur Team | 110 Down |
| Napalitano Team | 232 Down |

| Code | Enter |
|------|-------|
| Olshan Team | 222 Down |
| Pinto Team | 210 Right |
| Rivera Team | 222 Up |
| Rodeo Clown | 132 Down |
| Scorpion Team | 112 Down |
| Team Terry Fitzgerald | 333 Right |
| Team Todd McFarlane | 222 Right |
| Atlantis Stadium | 321 Left |
| Coliseum Stadium | 333 Up |
| Empire Park Stadium | 321 Right |
| Forbidden City Stadium | 333 Left |
| Midway Park Stadium | 321 Down |
| Monument Stadium | 333 Down |
| Rocket Park Stadium | 321 Up |

| | |
|------|-------|
| Extended Time for Codes | 303 Up |

# NAMCO MUSEUM VOL. I

### GALAGA
### Display Timer

At the Galaga title screen, press Left, Right, Left, Right, Up, Down, Up, Down.

### Pac Attack
### Passwords

| Level | Password |
|-------|----------|
| 1 | STR |
| 2 | HNM |
| 3 | KST |
| 4 | TRT |
| 5 | MYX |
| 6 | KHL |

| Level | Password |
|-------|----------|
| 7 | RTS |
| 8 | SKB |
| 9 | HNT |
| 10 | SRY |
| 11 | YSK |
| 12 | RCF |
| 13 | HSM |
| 14 | PWW |
| 15 | MTN |
| 16 | TKY |
| 17 | RGH |
| 18 | TNS |
| 19 | YKM |
| 20 | MWS |
| 21 | KTY |
| 22 | TYK |
| 23 | SMM |
| 24 | NFL |
| 25 | SRT |
| 26 | KKT |
| 27 | MDD |
| 28 | CWD |
| 29 | DRC |
| 30 | WHT |
| 31 | FLT |
| 32 | SKM |
| 33 | QTN |
| 34 | SMN |
| 35 | TGR |
| 36 | WKR |
| 37 | YYP |
| 38 | SLS |
| 39 | THD |
| 40 | RMN |
| 41 | CNK |
| 42 | FRB |
| 43 | MLR |
| 44 | FRP |
| 45 | SDB |
| 46 | BQJ |
| 47 | VSM |
| 48 | RDY |
| 49 | XPL |

| Level | Password |
|-------|----------|
| 50 | WLC |
| 51 | TMF |
| 52 | QNS |
| 53 | GWR |
| 54 | PLT |
| 55 | KRW |
| 56 | HRC |
| 57 | RPN |
| 58 | CNT |
| 59 | BTT |
| 60 | TMP |
| 61 | MNS |
| 62 | SWD |
| 63 | LDM |
| 64 | YST |
| 65 | OTM |
| 66 | BRP |
| 67 | MRS |
| 68 | PPY |
| 69 | SWT |
| 70 | WTM |
| 71 | FST |
| 72 | SLW |
| 73 | XWF |
| 74 | RGJ |
| 75 | SNC |
| 76 | BKP |
| 77 | CRN |
| 78 | XNT |
| 79 | RNT |
| 80 | BSK |
| 81 | JWK |
| 82 | GSN |
| 83 | MMT |
| 84 | DNK |
| 85 | HPN |
| 86 | DCR |
| 87 | BNS |
| 88 | SDC |
| 89 | MRH |
| 90 | BTF |
| 91 | NSM |
| 92 | QYZ |

| Level | Password |
|-------|----------|
| 93 | KTT |
| 94 | FGS |
| 95 | RRC |
| 96 | YLW |
| 97 | PNN |
| 98 | SPR |
| 99 | CHB |
| 100 | LST |

# NASCAR THUNDER 2004

### All Cameos

Select Create-A-Car from the Features menu and name your car Seymore Cameos.

# NBA 2K3

### Codes

Select Game Play from the Options menu, hold Left on the D-pad + Right on the Left Thumbstick, then press START. Exit to the Options screen and a Codes option will appear.

### Sega Sports, Visual Concepts and NBA 2K3 Teams

Enter MEGASTARS as a code.

### Street Trash

Enter SPRINGER as a code.

### Duotone Draw

Enter DUOTONE as a code.

# NBA INSIDE DRIVE 2003

Select Codes from the Options screen and enter the following. Re-enter a code to disable it.

**Unlimited Turbo**
Enter SPEEDY.

**Created Players All Points Available**
Enter MOMONEY.

**Easy Three-Pointers**
Enter THREE4ALL.

**Easy Alley Oops**
Enter DUNKONYOU.

**Tiny Players**
Enter ITSYBITSY.

**8-Ball**
Enter CORNERPOCKET.

**ABA Ball**
Enter STYLIN70S.

**Beach Ball**
Enter BEACHBUMS.

**Soccer Ball**
Enter KICKME.

**Volleyball**
Enter SPIKEIT.

**WNBA Ball**
Enter GOTGAME.

**Xbox Ball**
Enter XBALL.

**Chicago Skyline Stadium (Single Game)**

Enter CITYHOOPS.

**Accept All Trades**

Enter DOIT.

**Allow Hidden Players**

Enter PEEKABOO. Create a player with the following names for classic versions of each:

Patrick Ewing

Shawn Kemp

Michael Jordan

Karl Malone

Reggie Miller

Hakeem Olajuwon

Scottie Pippen

## NBA LIVE 2003

Select Roster Management from the Team Management menu, then create a player with the following last names. These characters will be available as free agents.

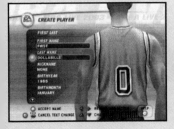

### B-Rich

Enter DOLLABILLS.

### Fabolous

Enter GHETTOFAB.

### Busta Rhymes

Enter FLIPMODE.

### Hot Karl

Enter CALIFORNIA.

### DJ Clue

Enter MIXTAPES.

### Just Blaze

Enter GOODBEATS.

# NBA STREET VOL. 2

Select Pick Up Game, hold L and enter the following codes when "Enter cheat codes now" appears at the bottom of the screen:

**Unlimited Turbo**

Press X, X, Y, Y.

**ABA Ball**

Press B, X, B, X.

**WNBA Ball**

Press B, Y, Y, B.

**No Display Bars**

Press X, B (x3).

**All Jerseys**

Press B, Y, X, X.

**All Courts**

Press X, Y, Y, X.

**St. Lunatics Team and All Street Legends**

Press X, Y, B, Y.

**All NBA Legends**

Press B, Y, Y, X.

**Classic Michael Jordan**
 Press B, Y, B, B.

**Explosive Rims**
 Press B (x3), Y.

**Small Players**
 Press Y, Y, B, X.

**Big Heads**
 Press B, X, X, B.

**No Counters**
 Press Y, Y, B, B.

**Ball Trails**
 Press Y, Y, Y, X.

**All Quicks**
 Press Y, B, Y, X.

**Easy Shots**
 Press Y, B, X, Y.

**Hard Shots**
 Press Y, X, B, Y.

# NICKELODEON PARTY BLAST

**Secret Characters**
 Select Blast and press Down, Down, Right, Left, Right, Up, Left, Down, Right.

**Clam Games**
 Select Blast and press Up, Up, Down, Down, Left, Right.

**Bungi Games**
 At the Game Select screen, highlight Bungi and press Up, Up, Down, Down, Left, Right.

# OUTLAW VOLLEYBALL

**All Characters and Costumes**
 Select exhibition, then at the character select, hold L and press Left, White, Right, White.

### All Courts

Select exhibition, then at the Court select, hold L and press Up, Down, Up, Down, Left, Left, Right, Right.

### Maximum Stats in Exhibition

Select exhibition, then at the character select, hold R and press Left, White, Right, White.

### Big Heads

During the game, hold L and quickly press B, A, B, Y during game play.

### Big Chests

Hold L and quickly press B, Up, Up, B, Y during game play.

### Mines in Exhibition

During the game, hold L and press A, B, B, Y, A + X.

# PHANTOM CRASH

### Invincibility

At the main menu, press X, Y, B, A, Back, White, Up, Down, Up, Down.

# PIRATES OF THE CARIBBEAN

### Invincibility

During a game, press A, Y, X, X, Y, Y, B, Y, X.

### 100,000 Gold

During a game, press A, X, Y, B, Y, B, X, B, B.

### 50 Skill Points

During a game, press A, B, Y, X, Y, B, B, Y, B.

### Neutral Reputation

During a game, press A, X, Y, X, Y, B, B, Y, B.

# PRO RACE DRIVER

Enter the following codes at the Bonus screen:

**Realistic Handling**
Enter SIM.

**Enhanced Damage**
Enter DAMAGE.

**Credits**
Enter CREDITS.

# QUANTUM REDSHIFT

Enter CHEAT as your name, then enter the following codes:

**All Characters**
Enter Nematode.

**All Speeds**
Enter zoomZOOM.

**Upgrade All Ships**
Enter RICEitup.

**Unlimited Turbo**
Enter FishFace.

**Infinite Shields**
Enter ThinkBat.

# RED FACTION II

Select Cheats from the Extras menu and enter the following codes:

**Unlock Everything**
Press White, White, X, X, Y, Black, Y, Black.

**All Cheats**
Press Y, Black, White, Black, Y, X, White, X.

### Level Select

Press Black, Y, X, White, Y, Black, X, X.

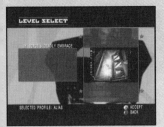

### Super Health

Press X, X, Y, White, Y, White, Black.

### Infinite Grenades

Press Black, X, Black, Y, X, Black, X, Black.

### Director's Cut

Press Y, X, Black, White, Black, X, Y, White.

### Rapid Rails

Press Black, Y, Black, Y, X, X, White, White.

### Extra Chunky

Press Black (x4), White, X, Black, Black.

### Infinite Ammo

Press Y, White, X, Black, Y, Black, X, White.

### Wacky Deaths

Press White (x8).

### Walking Dead

Press X (x8).

### Rain of Fire Cheat

Press Y (x8).

### Gibby Explosions

Press White, Black, X, Y, White, Black, X, Y.

### Explosive Personality

Press X.

## ROCKY

### Punch Double Damage

At the Main Menu, hold R and press Right, Down, Left, Up, Left, L.

### Double Speed Boxing

At the Main Menu, hold R and press Down, Left, Down, Up, Right, L.

### All Default Boxers and Arenas

At the Main Menu, hold R and press Right, Down, Up, Left, Up, L. This *doesn't* unlock Mickey or the Rocky Statue.

### All Default Boxers, Arenas, and Rocky Statue

At the Main Menu, hold R and press Right (x3), Left, Right, L.

### All Default Boxers, Arenas, Rocky Statue, and Mickey

At the Main Menu, hold R and press Up, Down, Down, Left, Left, L.

### Full Stats, Tournament and Exhibition Modes

At the Main Menu, hold R and press Left, Up, Up, Down, Right, L.

### Full Stats, Movie Mode

At the Main Menu, hold R and press Right, Down, Down, Up, Left, L.

### Win Fight, Movie Mode

At the Main Menu, hold R and press Right, Right, Left, Left, Up, L. During a fight, press Black + White to win.

# ROLLER COASTER TYCOON

Select a guest and change his/her name to one of the following:

**Photographer**

Enter Chris Sawyer.

**Artist**

Enter Simon Foster.

**Waving**

Enter Katie Brayshaw.

**"Wow!"**

Enter John Wardley.

# RUN LIKE HELL

Press Back during a game to bring up the inventory screen. Press L + R + Left Thumbstick + Right Thumbstick. Then enter the following:

**Nick Conner's Health**

Press Up, Down, Left, Right, Left, Right, A, B.

**Nick Conner's Armor**

Press A, Y, B, X, Y, A, Left Thumbstick, Right Thumbstick

**Baby Nick Conner**

Press B, A, B, Y, Down, Down.

**Max Assault Rifle Damage**

Press Left, B, Right, X, Down, Y, Up, A.

**Max Bolt Thrower Damage**

Press X, Y, B, White, B, Y, X, Black.

**Max Pulse Rifle Damage**

Press B, Down, Left, A, White, Black, X, Y

**Max Repeater Rifle Damage**

Press Left, Y, Right, A, Up, X, Down, B.

**Max Rifle Damage**

Press Left Thumbstick, Left Thumbstick, X, Y, B, A, Right Thumbstick, Right Thumbstick.

**Max Shotgun Damage**

Press A, A, Left Thumbstick, Right Thumbstick, Up, Down, Left, Right.

**Credits**

Press X, B, A, Up, Down, Y.

**Breaking Benjamin Music Video**

Press Left, B, A, L, R, Up.

# SCOOBY-DOO: NIGHT OF 100 FRIGHTS

**Movie Gallery**

Pause the game, hold L + R and press X, X, X, B, B, B, X, B, X.

**All Power-Ups**

Pause the game, hold L + R and press B, X, B, X, B, X, X, X, B, B, X, B, B, B.

**Alternate Credits**

Pause the game, hold L + R and press X, B, B, X, B, X.

**Holidays**

Change the system date to one of the following dates to change the appearance:

| | |
|---|---|
| January 1 | October 31 |
| July 4 | December 25 |

# SERIOUS SAM

### Cheats

At the Main Menu, click and hold the Left Thumbstick and press Black, White, Y.

# SPEED KINGS

Enter the following as your Handle:

### Lap Times – Unlock Grand Prix

Enter .LAPT18.

### Complete Driving Test

Enter .TEST9.

**All meets won**

Enter .MEET6.

**Respect Points**

Enter .Resp ##. Replace ## with the desired amount of respect.

**Master Cheat**

Enter borkbork as a name.

# SPLINTER CELL

**Level Select**

Enter !LAMAUDITE! as a Profile Name.

# STARSKY AND HUTCH

**Unlock Everything**

Enter VADKRAM as a profile name.

# STAR WARS JEDI KNIGHT II: JEDI OUTCAST

Select Cheats from the Extras menu to enter the following codes:

**Invulnerable**
Enter BUBBLE.

**Inifinite Ammo**
Enter BISCUIT.

**All Characters in Jedi Arena**
Enter PEEPS.

**Start with Lightsaber**
Enter FUDGE.

**All FMVs**
Enter FLICKY.

**Level Select**
Enter CHERRY.

# STAR WARS: JEDI STARFIGHTER

Select Codes from the Options screen to enter the following:

**Unlock Everything**
Enter LONGO.

**Headhunter Ship**
Enter HUNTER.

**Invincible**
Enter ARTOO.

**No HUD**
Enter CONVISTA.

**Jar Jar Mode**
Enter JARJAR.

**Director Mode**
Enter DARON.

# STAR WARS: KNIGHTS OF THE OLD REPUBLIC

### High Pitch Voices

Plug another controller into the fourth port and press the White Button.

### Low Pitch Voices

Plug another controller into the fourth port and press the Black Button.

# STAR WARS: THE CLONE WARS

Select Bonuses from the Options menu, then select Codes to enter the following:

### Unlimited Ammo

Enter NOHONOR.

### All Multiplayer Maps

Enter LETSDANCE.

### Team Photos

Enter YOURMASTERS.

### All Cutscenes

Enter GOTPOPCORN.

### Three Bonus Objectives

Enter ALITTLEHELP.

### All Bonus Menu Items

Enter IGIVEUP.

# STATE OF EMERGENCY

### Invulnerable

During gameplay, press White, L, Black, R, A.

### Unlimited Ammo

During gameplay, press White, L, Black, R, Y.

### Complete Current Mission

During gameplay, press Left (x4), Y.

### Infinite Time in Chaos Mode

During gameplay, press White, L, Black, R, B.

### Little Player

During gameplay, press Black, R, White, L, A.

### Big Player

During gameplay, press Black, R, White, L, Y.

### Normal Player

During gameplay, press Black, R, White, L, B.

### Punches Decapitate

During gameplay, press White, L, Black, R, X.

## Looting on the Rise

During gameplay, press
Black, White, R, L, Y.

## Bull

During gameplay, press
Right (x4), A.

## Freak

During gameplay, press
Right (x4), B.

## Spanky

During gameplay, press
Right (x4), Y.

## AK-47

During gameplay, press
Left, Right, Down, R, Y.

## Flamethrower

During gameplay, press
Left, Right, Down, Black, B.

## Grenade

During gameplay, press
Left, Right, Down, R, X.

## Grenade Launcher

During gameplay, press
Left, Right, Down, Black, X.

## M-16

During gameplay, press
Left, Right, Down, R, B.

## Minigun

During gameplay, press
Left, Right, Down, Black, Y.

## Molotov Cocktail

During gameplay, press
Left, Right, Down, R, A.

### Pepper Spray

During gameplay, press Left, Right, Down, White, X.

### Pistol

During gameplay, press Left, Right, Down, White, Y.

### Rocket Launcher

During gameplay, press Left, Right, Down, Black, A.

### Shotgun

During gameplay, press Left, Right, Down, L, Y.

### Tazer

During gameplay, press Left, Right, Down, White, B.

### Tear Gas

During gameplay, press Left, Right, Down, White, A.

# STEEL BATTALION

### All VTs and Levels in Free Mission Mode

At the Title screen, use the tuner and point it at the following numbers (in order) for one second each:

1, 9, 7, 9, 0, 9, 0, 6

# SUPERMAN: THE MAN OF STEEL

### All Levels and Bonuses

Pause the game and press R, Black, Y, Black, L, White.

### Unlimited Health

Pause the game and press Black, White, L, X, L, White.

### X-Ray Graphics

Pause the game and press L, L, R, L, Y, X, White, Black, Black, White.

### Freeze Graphics

Pause the game and press R, L, Black, White, L, Y, Y, Black, R, White.

# THE ELDER SCROLLS III: MORROWIND

During gameplay, access the Options screen. Go to the Statistics page to enter the following codes. You can only enter one code at a time.

### Restore Health

Highlight Health and press Black, White, Black (x3). Hold A until you reach a desired level.

### Restore Magicka

Highlight Magicka and press Black, White, White, Black, White. Hold A until you reach a desired level.

### Restore Fatigue

Highlight Fatigue and press Black, Black, White, White, Black. Hold A until you reach a desired level.

# THE GREAT ESCAPE

### Level Select and The Greatest Escape Mode

At the main menu, press Y, R, Y, X, Y, R, X, L, X (x3), Y.

### Play All Movies

At the main menu, press L, L, Y, X, X, R, R, Y, Y, X, L, R. Press A to skip to the next movie.

### Unlimited Ammo

Pause the game and press Y, X, L, R, L, R, X, Y, L, Y, Y, R.

# THE LORD OF THE RINGS: THE TWO TOWERS

### Health

Pause the game, hold L + R and press Y, Down, A, Up.

### Arrows

Pause the game, hold L + R and press A, Down, Y, Up.

### 1000 Upgrade Points

Pause the game, hold L + R and press A, Down (x3).

### Level 2 Skills

Pause the game, hold L + R and press B, Right, B, Right.

### Level 4 Skills

Pause the game, hold L + R and press Y, Up, Y, Up.

### Level 6 Skills

Pause the game, hold L + R and press X, Left, X, Left.

### Level 8 Skills

Pause the game, hold L + R and press A, A, Down, Down.

You must first complete the game to enter the following codes:

### Always Devastating

Pause the game, hold L + R and press X, X, B, B.

### Small Enemies

Pause the game, hold L + R and press Y, Y, A, A.

### All Upgrades

Pause the game, hold L + R and press Y, B, Y, B.

### Invulnerable

Pause the game, hold L + R and press Y, X, A, B.

### Slow Motion

Pause the game, hold L + R and press Y, B, A, X.

### Unlimited Missile Weapons

Pause the game, hold L + R and press X, B, A, Y.

## THE SIMPSONS: HIT & RUN

Select the Options from the main menu, hold L + R and enter the following:

**Red Brick Car**

Enter B, B, Y, X.

**Fast Cars**

Enter X, X, X, X.

**Faster Cars**

Enter Y, Y, Y, Y.

**One-Hit Wreck**

Enter Y, Y, X, X.

**Use Horn to Jump in Car**

Enter X, X, X, Y.

**Show Speed**

Enter Y, Y, B, X.

**Change Camera**

Enter B, B, B, A.

**Grid View**

Enter B, A, B, Y.

**Trippy**

Enter Y, B, Y, B.

**Credits Dialog**

Enter A, X, X, Y.

**Holiday Decorated Living Room**

Change the date of your system to Thanksgiving, Halloween or Christmas for a new look.

# THE SIMS

At the Main Menu, press L + R, then enter the following codes:

**Play The Sims Mode, All 2-Player Games, Objects, and Skins**

Enter MIDAS. Select Get A Life and start a new game. Join Roxy in the hot tub, pause the game and quit.

**The Party Motel 2-Player Game**

Enter PARTY M.

**First-Person View**

Enter FISH EYE. Press B to toggle the view.

## TIGER WOODS PGA TOUR 2004

Select Password from the Options menu and enter the following:

### All Golfers and Courses
Enter THEKITCHENSINK.

### All Golfers
Enter CANYOUPICKONE

### All Courses
Enter ALLTHETRACKS.

### Target® World Challenge
Enter SHERWOOD TARGET.

### Sunday Tiger Woods
Enter 4REDSHIRTS.

### Cedric "Ace" Andrews
Enter ACEINTHEHOLE.

### Felicia "Downtown" Brown
Enter DTBROWN.

**Dominic "The Don" Donatello**
Enter DISCOKING.

**Cedric The Entertainer**
Enter CEDDYBEAR.

**Solita Lopez**
Enter SHORTGAME.

**Edwin "Pops" Masterson**
Enter EDDIE.

**Hamish "Mulligan" McGregor**
Enter DWILBY.

**Takeharu "Tsunami" Moto**
Enter EMERALDCHAMP.

**Kellie Newman**
Enter TRAVELER.

**Val "Sunshine" Summers**
Enter BEVERLYHILLS.

**Moa "Big Mo" Ta'a Vatu**
Enter ERUPTION.

**Melvin "Yosh" Tanigawa**
Enter THENEWLEFTY.

**Erika "Ice" Von Severin**
Enter ICYONE.

# TOM CLANCY'S GHOST RECON

After completing all of the objectives, you can enter the following cheats. During gameplay, press Black and enter the following:

**Team Invincibility**
Press B, A, Y, Y, A, B, X (x3).

**Big Heads**
Press A, X, B, Y, A.

**Paper Mode**

Press B, A, X, Y, A.

**Chicken Explosives**

Press X, X, Y, A, B.

**High-Pitched Voices**

Press X, A, Y, B, X.

**Slow Motion**

Press Y, Y, B, X, A.

# TOM CLANCY'S GHOST RECON: ISLAND THUNDER

Before you can use the following codes you must complete all objectives in the single mission dossiers. Pause the game, select Enter Cheats then enter the following:

**Invincibility**

Press X, X, A, B, A.

**Run Faster**

Press A, A, X, B, Y.

**Slow Motion**

Press Y, Y, B, X, A.

**Chicken Explosives**

Press X, X, Y, A, B.

**Big Heads**

Press A, X, B, Y, A.

**Big Bodies**

Press B, B, Y, X, X, A.

**Paper Mode**

Press B, A, X, Y, A.

**High Pitched Voices**

Press X, A, Y, B, X.

# TONY HAWK'S PRO SKATER 4

Select Cheat Codes from the Options screen to enter the following codes:

171

### Unlock Everything

Enter **watch_me_xplode**. You must turn on the cheats by selecting Cheats from the Options screen during gameplay.

### Daisy

Enter **(o)(o)**.

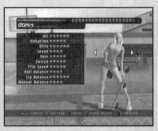

### Moon Gravity

Enter **moon$hot**.

### Always Special

Enter **i'myellow**.

### Perfect Rail

Enter **belikeeric**.

### Perfect Skitch

Enter **bumperrub**.

### Stats 13

Enter **4p0sers**.

### Perfect Manual

Enter **freewheelie**.

### Matrix Mode

Enter **fbiagent**.

### Secret Created Skaters

Enter the following names for hidden created skaters:

#$%@!
Aaron Skillman
Adam Lippmann
Andrew Skates
Andy Marchal
Angus
Atiba Jefferson
Ben Scott Pye
Big Tex

Brian Jennings
Captain Liberty
Chauwa Steel
Chris Peacock
ConMan
Danaconda
Dave Stohl
DDT
DeadEndRoad
Fritz
Gary Jesdanun
grjost
Henry Ji

Jason Uyeda
Jim Jagger
Joe Favazza
John Rosser
Jow
Kenzo
Kevin Mulhall
Kraken
Lindsey Hayes
Lisa G Davies

Little Man
Marilena Rixfor
Mat Hoffman
Matt Mcpherson
Maya's Daddy
Meek West
Mike Day
Mike Lashever
Mike Ward
Mr. Brad
Nolan Nelson
Parking Guy

Peasus

Pete Day

Pooper

Rick Thorne

Sik

Stacey D

Stacey Ytuarte

Team Chicken

Ted Barber

Todd Wahoske

Top Bloke

Wardcore

Zac ZiG Drake

# WAKEBOARDING UNLEASHED

At the Main Menu, enter the following codes. You should get the corresponding message when the code is entered correctly.

## Boards 2 and 3

Message: YOU GOT ALL THE BOARDS... OR DID YOU?

Press Up, Up, Left, Left, Right, Right, Down, Down, Up, Left, Right, Down, Up, Left, Right, Down.

## All Levels

Message: TRAVEL VISA APPROVED

Press X (x4), A (x4), Y (x4), X, A, Y.

## 100% of Everything

Message: ULTIMATE CHEAT...

Press Up, Down, Up, Down, Up, Down, Up, Down, Up, Down, Left, Right, Left, Right, Left, Right, Left, Right, Left, Right.

# X2: WOLVERINE'S REVENGE

## Unlock Everything

At the Main Menu, press X, L, X, L, X, X, L, R, X, L, X, L, X, X, L, R.

## Level Select & All Challenges

At the Main Menu, press X, L, X, L, X, L, L, R.

## All Cerebro Files and Movies

At the Main Menu, press X, L, X, L, X, X, R, L.

## All Costumes

At the Main Menu, press X, L, X, L, X, X, L, R.

## Cheats

At the Main Menu, press X, X, L (x4), X, X, L. Pause the game to find the Cheats.

# X-MEN: NEXT DIMENSION

## Unlock All

At the Main Menu, hold L and press Right, Right, Left, Left, Down, Up, B.

# Games List

ATV QUAD POWER RACING 2 . . . . . . . . . . . . . . . .178

BALDUR'S GATE: DARK ALLIANCE . . . . . . . . . . . .178

BEACH SPIKERS . . . . . . . . . . . . . . . . . . . . . . . . . .179

BIG MUTHA TRUCKERS . . . . . . . . . . . . . . . . . . . .181

BLACK AND BRUISED . . . . . . . . . . . . . . . . . . . . . .181

CONFLICT: DESERT STORM . . . . . . . . . . . . . . . . . .182

CUBIX: ROBOTS FOR EVERYONE SHOWDOWN . .182

DAKAR 2: THE WORLD'S ULTIMATE RALLY . . . . . .183

DEAD TO RIGHTS . . . . . . . . . . . . . . . . . . . . . . . . .183

DEF JAM VENDETTA . . . . . . . . . . . . . . . . . . . . . . .184

DIE HARD: VENDETTA . . . . . . . . . . . . . . . . . . . . . .187

DR. MUTO . . . . . . . . . . . . . . . . . . . . . . . . . . . . . .189

ENTER THE MATRIX . . . . . . . . . . . . . . . . . . . . . . .189

EVOLUTION SKATEBOARDING . . . . . . . . . . . . . . .189

FINDING NEMO . . . . . . . . . . . . . . . . . . . . . . . . . .190

FREEDOM FIGHTERS . . . . . . . . . . . . . . . . . . . . . .191

GODZILLA: DESTROY ALL MONSTERS MELEE . . . .192

HULK . . . . . . . . . . . . . . . . . . . . . . . . . . . . . . . . . .194

JAMES BOND 007: NIGHTFIRE . . . . . . . . . . . . . . .195

LEGACY OF KAIN: BLOOD OMEN 2 . . . . . . . . . . .197

LORD OF THE RINGS: THE TWO TOWERS . . . . . .198

MAT HOFFMAN'S PRO BMX 2 . . . . . . . . . . . . . . .199

MEDAL OF HONOR: FRONTLINE . . . . . . . . . . . . .201

MEN IN BLACK 2: ALIEN ESCAPE . . . . . . . . . . . . .202

MINORITY REPORT . . . . . . . . . . . . . . . . . . . . . . .203

MLB SLUGFEST 20-04 . . . . . . . . . . . . . . . . . . . . .205

NASCAR: DIRT TO DAYTONA . . . . . . . . . . . . . . .208

NBA 2K3 . . . . . . . . . . . . . . . . . . . . . . . . . . . . . . .208

NBA LIVE 2003 . . . . . . . . . . . . . . . . . . . . . . . . . .208

# GameCube™

NBA STREET VOL. 2 . . . . . . . . . . . . . . . . . . . . . . . .208

RED FACTION II . . . . . . . . . . . . . . . . . . . . . . . . . .210

ROBOTECH: BATTLECRY . . . . . . . . . . . . . . . . . . . .211

ROCKY . . . . . . . . . . . . . . . . . . . . . . . . . . . . . . . .212

SHOX . . . . . . . . . . . . . . . . . . . . . . . . . . . . . . . . .212

SONIC MEGA COLLECTION . . . . . . . . . . . . . . . . . .212

SPEED KINGS . . . . . . . . . . . . . . . . . . . . . . . . . . . .214

STAR WARS BOUNTY HUNTER . . . . . . . . . . . . . . .214

STAR WARS: THE CLONE WARS . . . . . . . . . . . . . . .214

STAR WARS JEDI KNIGHT II: JEDI OUTCAST . . . .216

STREET HOOPS . . . . . . . . . . . . . . . . . . . . . . . . . .217

SUPERMAN: SHADOW OF APOKOLIPS . . . . . . . .217

THE SIMPSONS: HIT & RUN . . . . . . . . . . . . . . . . .218

THE SIMPSONS: ROAD RAGE . . . . . . . . . . . . . . . .218

THE SIMS . . . . . . . . . . . . . . . . . . . . . . . . . . . . . . .220

TIGER WOODS PGA TOUR 2004 . . . . . . . . . . . . .221

TONY HAWK'S PRO SKATER 4 . . . . . . . . . . . . . . .222

TY THE TASMANIAN TIGER . . . . . . . . . . . . . . . . .224

V-RALLY 3 . . . . . . . . . . . . . . . . . . . . . . . . . . . . . . .225

WRECKLESS . . . . . . . . . . . . . . . . . . . . . . . . . . . . .225

WWE CRUSH HOUR . . . . . . . . . . . . . . . . . . . . . .225

X2: WOLVERINE'S REVENGE . . . . . . . . . . . . . . . . .226

X-MEN: NEXT DIMENSION . . . . . . . . . . . . . . . . .226

# ATV QUAD POWER RACING 2

**All Riders**

Enter BUBBA as a profile name.

**All Vehicles**

Enter GENERALLEE as a profile name.

**All Tracks**

Enter ROADKILL as a profile name.

**All Championships**

Enter REDROOSTER as a profile name.

**All Challenges**

Enter DOUBLEBARREL as a profile name.

**Maxed Out Skill Level**

Enter FIDDLERSELBOW as a profile name.

**Maxed Out Stats**

Enter GINGHAM as a profile name.

# BALDUR'S GATE: DARK ALLIANCE

**All Spells**

During gameplay, hold X + Right + L all the way + R halfway.

**Invincibility and Level Warp**

During gameplay, hold Y + Left + L all the way + R halfway and, then press START.

# BEACH SPIKERS

### Uniforms

In World Tour, name your player one of the following to unlock bonus outfits. The name disappears when entered correctly.

| Name | Uniforms |
| --- | --- |
| JUSTICE | 105-106, Sunglasses 94 |

| DAYTONA | 107-108 |
| --- | --- |

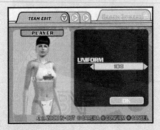

| Name | Uniforms |
|------|----------|

**FVIPERS** — 109-110, Face 51, Hair 75

**ARAKATA** — 111-113, Face 52, Hair 76

**PHANTA2** — 114-115, Face 53, Hair 77

**OHTORII** — 116-117

# BIG MUTHA TRUCKERS

**All Cheats**
Enter CHEATING MUTHATRUCKER as a code.

**Evil Truck**
Enter VARLEY as a code.

**Fast Truck**
Enter GINGERBEER as a code.

**$10 Million**
Enter LOTSAMONEY as a code.

**Level Select**
Enter LAZYPLAYER as a code.

**Unlimited Time**
Enter PUBLICTRANS PORT as a code.

**Disable Damage**
Enter 6WL as a code.

**Automatic Sat Nav**
Enter USETHEFORCE as a code.

**Diplomatic Immunity**
Enter VICTORS as a code.

**Small Pedestrians**
Enter DAISHI as a code.

**Bonus Levels**
Enter JINGLEBELLS as a code in the options screen.

# BLACK AND BRUISED

**Intercontinental Mode**
Select Cheat Codes from the Setup menu and press START, A (x3), Y (x3), X (x3), START.

**Second Skin**
Select Cheat Codes from the Setup menu and press START, A, Z, Y, X, START.

**All Boxers**
Select Cheat Codes from the Setup menu and press START, A, Y, X, X, Z, Z, X, Y, A, START.

**Scrap Yard Scene**
Select Cheat Codes from the Setup menu and press START, Y, Z, Y, Z, A, A, START.

### Conversation Mode

Select Cheat Codes from the Setup menu and press START, Z, A, Y, X, Z (x3), START.

### Invulnerability

Select Cheat Codes from the Setup menu and press START, A, A, Y, Y, Z, Z, X, X, START. Enter the code with Controller 2 for Invulnerability for Boxer 2.

### All Boxers' Life

Select Cheat Codes from the Setup menu and press START, A, X, Y, Z, A, X, Y, Z, START.

### Double Speed

Select Cheat Codes from the Setup menu and press START, Z (x10), START.

### Constant Power-Up

Select Cheat Codes from the Setup menu and press START, A, Y, A, Y, A, Y, X (x3), START. Enter the code with Controller 2 to get Constant Power-up for Boxer 2.

# CONFLICT: DESERT STORM

### Cheat Mode

At the main menu, press Left, Left, Right, Right, Up, Up, Down, Down, X, X, Y, Y. Pause the game to find the Cheats option.

# CUBIX: ROBOTS FOR EVERYONE SHOWDOWN

Select Cheats from the Extras menu and enter the following:

**Complete Game as Abby**
Press X, R, X, Y, X, Y, R, L.

**Complete Game as Connor**
Press X, Y, L, Y, X, Y, L, R.

**Dr. K's Base Robots**
Press Z, A, Y (x3), X, A.

**Construction Robots**
Press Y (x4), Z, A, R.

**Bubble Town Day Robots**
Press Y, Y, Z, Y, Y, R, L.

**Bubble Town Night Robots**
Press Y, L, Y, Y, X, L, Z.

# DAKAR 2: THE WORLD'S ULTIMATE RALLY

Select Cheat Code from the Extras menu and enter the following:

**All Vehicles**
Enter SWEETAS

**All Tracks**
Enter BONZER

# DEAD TO RIGHTS

From the Main Menu, hold L + R and enter the following cheats:

**Lazy Mode**
Press Down, Left, Down, Y, Down.

**10,000 Bullets Mode**
Press Up, Left, Down, Right, X.

**Time To Play**
Press B, B, X, X, Right.

**One-Shot Kill**
Press Y, X, X, X, Left.

**Sharpshooter Mode**
Press B, B, B, Down, Right.

**Bang Bang**
Press X, Y, B, X, Right.

**Precursor**
Press Up, Up, Down, Down, Up.

**Super Cop Mode**
Press B, Y, Left, Up, Right.

**Infinite Stamina**
Press X, B, Y, X, Down.

**Infinite Adrenaline**
Left, Right, Left, X, B.

**Bulletproof Mode**
Press Up, Up, Up, B, Down.

**Chow Yun Jack Mode**
Press Y, X, Up, Up, Up.

**Up Close and Personal Mode**
Press B, Y, X, Y, B.

**Extraordinary Skills**
Press X, X, Up, Up, B.

**Fight Club**
Press Right, B, Left, X, Y.

**Invisible Jack Mode**
Press Y, Y, Up, Up, Y.

**Boomstick Mode**
Press Right, X, X, X, B.

**Hard Boiled Mode**
Press Y, B, Left, Left, X.

**Wussy Mode**
Press B, Left, Y, Up, Down.

# DEF JAM: VENDETTA

**Arii**
At the Character Select screen, hold L + R + Z and press A, Y, B, X, Y.

**Carla**
At the Character Select screen, hold L + R + Z and press A, Y, A (x3).

**Chukklez**
At the Character Select screen, hold L + R + Z and press Y, Y, B, A, X.

**Cruz**
At the Character Select screen, hold L + R + Z and press X, B, A, A, X.

**D-Mob**
At the Character Select screen, hold L + R + Z and press Y, Y, B, Y, Y.

## Dan G

At the Character Select screen, hold L + R + Z and press A, X, A, X, Y.

## Deebo

At the Character Select screen, hold L + R + Z and press X, X, A, A, B.

## Deja

At the Character Select screen, hold L + R + Z and press X, Y, X, X, A.

## DMX

At the Character Select screen, hold L + R + Z and press X, A, X, B, Y.

## Drake

At the Character Select screen, hold L + R + Z and press A, B, B, X, X.

## Funkmaster Flex

At the Character Select screen, hold L + R + Z and press X, B, X, X, Y.

## Headache

At the Character Select screen, hold L + R + Z and press B (x3), Y, X.

## House

At the Character Select screen, hold L + R + Z and press B, A, B, X, A.

## Iceberg

At the Character Select screen, hold L + R + Z and press Y, B, X, Y, X.

## Ludacris

At the Character Select screen, hold L + R + Z and press X (x3), Y, B.

## Masa

At the Character Select screen, hold L + R + Z and press A, X, B, Y, Y.

## Method Man

At the Character Select screen, hold L + R + Z and press Y, X, A, B, X.

## Moses

At the Character Select screen, hold L + R + Z and press B, B, Y, Y, A.

## N.O.R.E.

At the Character Select screen, hold L + R + Z and press X, Y, B, A, X.

### Nyne

At the Character Select screen, hold L + R + Z and press Y, X, A, A, B.

### Opal

At the Character Select screen, hold L + R + Z and press X, X, Y, Y, B.

### Peewee

At the Character Select screen, hold L + R + Z and press A, A, Y, B, Y.

### Ruffneck

At the Character Select screen, hold L + R + Z and press A, Y, A, B, X.

### Scarface

At the Character Select screen, hold L + R + Z and press X, Y, A, B, Y.

### Sketch

At the Character Select screen, hold L + R + Z and press B, B, X, Y, A.

### Penny

At the Character Select screen, hold L + R + Z and press A (x3), B, X.

### Pockets

At the Character Select screen, hold L + R + Z and press B, Y, X, Y, A.

### Razor

At the Character Select screen, hold L + R + Z and press B, Y, B, X, A.

### Redman

At the Character Select screen, hold L + R + Z and press X, X, B, Y, A.

### Snowman

At the Character Select screen, hold L + R + Z and press B, B, A, A, X.

### Steel

At the Character Select screen, hold L + R + Z and press A, B, X, X, B.

### T'ai

At the Character Select screen, hold L + R + Z and press X, X, Y, A, X.

### Zaheer

At the Character Select screen, hold L + R + Z and press B, B, Y, A, A.

### Alternate Costume, Briggs

At the Character Select screen, hold L + R + Z and press A, B, X, Y, X.

### Alternate Costume, Manny

At the Character Select screen, hold L + R + Z and press X, Y, X, Y, X.

### Alternate Costume, Proof

At the Character Select screen, hold L + R + Z and press A, Y, B, Y, X.

### Alternate Costume, Razor

At the Character Select screen, hold L + R + Z and press Y, X, A, B, B.

### Alternate Costume, Ruffneck

At the Character Select screen, hold L + R + Z and press Y, X, B, A, Y.

### Alternate Costume, Spider

At the Character Select screen, hold L + R + Z and press X, X, Y, B, B.

### Alternate Costume, Tank

At the Character Select screen, hold L + R + Z and press B, Y, X, A, A.

## DIE HARD: VENDETTA

Enter the following codes at the Main Menu. A message appears when the code is correctly entered.

### Invulnerable

At the Main Menu, press L, R, L, R, L, R, L, R.

## All Levels

At the Main Menu, press X, Y, Z, Z, X, Y, Z, Z.

## Flame On

At the Main Menu, press B, X, Y, B, X, Y.

## Infinite Hero Time

At the Main Menu, press B, X, Y, Z, L, R.

## Liquid Metal

At the Main Menu, press B, Y, X, B, Y, X.

## Big Heads

At the Main Menu, press R, R, L, R.

## Pin Heads

At the Main Menu, press L, L, R, L.

## Exploding Fists

At the Main Menu, press R, R, Y, B, X, R, R.

## Hot Fists

At the Main Menu, press L, L, X, B, Y, L, L.

## Kamikaze

At the Main Menu, press L, R, Z, Y, B.

# DR. MUTO

Select Cheats from the Options menu and enter the following:

**Invincibility**
Enter NECROSCI.
Invincibility doesn't work when falling from high above.

**Never Take Damage**
Enter CHEATERBOY.

**Unlock Every Gadget**
Enter TINKERTOY.

**Unlock Every Morph**
Enter EUREKA.

**Go Anywhere**
Enter BEAMMEUP.

**Secret Morphs**
Enter LOGGLOGG.

**See Movies**
Enter HOTTICKET.

**Super Ending**
Enter BUZZOFF.

# ENTER THE MATRIX

## Cheat Mode

After playing through the hacking system and unlocking CHEAT.EXE, you can use CHEAT.EXE to enter the following:

| Effect | Code |
| --- | --- |
| All Guns | 0034AFFF |
| Infinite Ammo | 1DDF2556 |
| Invisibility | FFFFFFF1 |
| Infinite Focus | 69E5D9E4 |
| Infinite Health | 7F4DF451 |
| Speedy Logos | 7867F443 |
| Unlock Secret Level | 13D2C77F |
| Fast Focus Restore | FFF0020A |
| Test Level | 13D2C77F |
| Enemies Can't Hear You | 4516DF45 |
| Turbo Mode | FF00001A |
| Multiplayer Fight | D5C55D1E |
| Low Gravity | BB013FFF |
| Taxi Driving | 312MF451 |

# EVOLUTION SKATEBOARDING

## All Secret Characters

When the Konami logo appears on-screen, press Up, Up, Down, Down, Left, Right, Left, Right, B, A, B, A, Start.

# FINDING NEMO

Enter the following at the main menu. The word Cheat! will appear if entered correctly. Pause the game at the level select to access the cheats.

## Level Select

Press Y (x3), B, B, X, B, Y, X, B, Y, B, Y, B, Y, X, Y, Y.

## Invincibility

Press Y, B, B, X (x3), Y, Y, B (x3), X (x4), B, Y, X (x3), B, X, Y, X, X, B, X, X, Y, X, B, X (x3), Y.

## Credits

Press Y, B, X, Y, Y, B, X, Y, B, X, Y, B, B, X, Y, B, X, Y, B, X, X, Y, B, X.

**Secret Level**

Press Y, B, X, X, B, Y, Y, B, X, X, B, Y, Y, X, B, Y, B, X, X, B, Y.

# FREEDOM FIGHTERS

**Cheat List**

During the game, enter the following:

| | |
|---|---|
| **Invisibility** | Y, A, X, B, B, Left |
| **Infinite ammo** | Y, A, X, B, A, Right |
| **Max charisma** | Y, A, X, B, A, Down |
| **Heavy machine gun** | Y, A, X, B, Y, Down |
| **Nail gun** | Y, A, X, B, A, Left |
| **Rocket launcher** | Y, A, X, B, Y, Left |
| **Shotgun** | Y, A, X, B, B, Up |
| **Sniper rifle** | Y, A, X, B, Y, Right |
| **Sub machine gun** | Y, A, X, B, Y, Up |
| **Ragdolls** | Y, A, X, B, X, Up |
| **Slow motion** | Y, A, X, B, B, Right |
| **Fast motion** | Y, A, X, B, B, Down |
| **Change spawn point** | Y, A, X, B, A, Up |

# GODZILLA: DESTROY ALL MONSTERS MELEE

## Codes

At the Main Menu, press and hold L, B, R, then release B, R, L. Enter the following codes:

| Effect | Code |
| --- | --- |
| All Cites | 480148 |
| All Monsters (except Orga) | 696924 |

| Godzilla 2K | 225133 |
| --- | --- |
| Gigan | 616233 |
| King Ghidorah | 877467 |
| Rodan | 104332 |
| Destoroyah | 537084 |
| Mecha King Ghidorah | 557456 |
| Mecha Godzilla | 131008 |
| 11 Continues | 760611 |
| Throw All Buildings & Objects | 756287 |
| P2 Invisible | 459113 |

| Effect | Code |
| --- | --- |
| All Players Invisible | 316022 |

| | |
| --- | --- |
| Player Indicators Always On | 135984 |
| Indestructible Buildings | 112122 |
| Turn Military On/Off | 256806 |
| Infinite Energy for P1 | 677251 |
| Infinite Energy for P2 | 435976 |
| No Freeze Tanks | 841720 |
| No Display | 443253 |
| No Energy (but stronger) | 650867 |
| No Health Power-ups | 562142 |
| No Mothra Power-ups | 134615 |
| No Energy Power-ups | 413403 |
| No Rage Power-ups | 119702 |
| P1 Always Rage | 649640 |
| P2 Always Rage | 122224 |
| P3 Always Rage | 548053 |
| P4 Always Rage | 451242 |
| P1 Damage-Proof | 843901 |
| P2 Damage-Proof | 706149 |
| P3 Damage-Proof | 188522 |
| P4 Damage-Proof | 286552 |
| All Players Damage-Proof | 505634 |
| Super Energy P1 | 677251 |
| Super Energy P2 | 435976 |
| Super Energy P3 | 603696 |
| Super Energy P4 | 291680 |
| Energy | 650867 |
| P1 4X Damage | 511012 |
| P2 4x Damage | 815480 |
| P3 4x Damage | 212454 |
| P4 4x Damage | 286552 |
| All Players 4x Damage | 817683 |
| P1 Small | 986875 |
| P2 Small | 971934 |
| P3 Small | 895636 |

| Effect | Code |
|--------|------|
| P4 Small | 795735 |
| All Players Small | 174204 |
| Regenerate Health | 492877 |
| Statistics Mode | 097401 |
| Black-and-White | 567980 |
| Technicolor | 661334 |
| View Credits | 176542 |
| Game Version | 097401 |

# HULK

## Cheat Codes

Select Code Input from the Options and enter the following and press Accept. Turn on the cheats by selecting Cheats from the Special Features menu.

| Description | Code Input |
|-------------|------------|
| Invulnerability | GMMSKIN |
| Regenerator | FLSHWND |
| Unlimited Continues | GRNCHTR |
| Double Hulk HP | HLTHDSE |
| Double Enemies HP | BRNGITN |
| Half Enemies HP | MMMYHLP |
| Reset High Score | NMBTHIH |
| Full Rage Meter | ANGMNGT |
| Puzzle Solved | BRCESTN |
| Wicked Punch | FSTOFRY |
| Unlock All Levels | TRUBLVR |

## Universal Unlock Codes

Enter the following at the special terminals, called "Universal Code Input," that are found throughout the levels. You will find these bonus materials in the Special Features menu.

| Play as Gray Hulk | JANITOR |
|-------------------|---------|
| Desert Battle Art | FIFTEEN |
| Hulk Movie FMV Art | NANOMED |
| Hulk Transformed ART | SANFRAN |
| Hulk vs. Hulk Dogs Art | PITBULL |

## JAMES BOND 007: NIGHTFIRE

Select Codenames from the Main Menu and pick a codename. Choose Secret Unlocks and enter the following codes. Save your codename before exiting this menu.

**Level Select**
Enter PASSPORT.

**Alpine Escape Level**
Enter POWDER.

**Enemies Vanquished Level**
Enter TRACTION.

**Double Cross Level**
Enter BONSAI.

**Night Shift Level**
Enter HIGHRISE.

**Chain Reaction Level**
Enter MELTDOWN.

**Phoenix Fire Level**
Enter FLAME.

**Deep Descent Level**
Enter AQUA.

**Island Infiltration Level**
Enter PARADISE.

**Countdown Level**
Enter BLASTOFF.

**Equinox Level**
Enter VACUUM.

**All Gadget Upgrades**
Enter Q LAB.

**Camera Upgrade**
Enter SHUTTER.

**Decrypter Upgrade**
Enter SESAME.

**Grapple Upgrade**
Enter LIFTOFF.

**Laser Upgrade**
Enter PHOTON.

**Scope Upgrade**
Enter SCOPE.

**Stunner Upgrade**
Enter ZAP.

**Tranquilizer Dart Upgrade**
Enter SLEEPY.

**Bigger Clip for Sniper Rifle**
Enter MAGAZINE.

**P2K Upgrade**
Enter P2000.

**Golden Wolfram P2K**
Enter AU P2K.

**Golden PP7**
Enter AU PP7.

**Vanquish Car Missile Upgrade**
Enter LAUNCH.

**All Multiplayer Scenarios**
Enter GAMEROOM.

**Uplink Multiplayer Scenario**
Enter TRANSMIT.

**Demolition Multiplayer Scenario**
Enter TNT.

**Protection Multiplayer Scenario**
Enter GUARDIAN.

**GoldenEye Strike Multiplayer Scenario**
Enter ORBIT.

**Assassination Multiplayer Scenario**
Enter TARGET.

**Team King of the Hill Multiplayer Scenario**
Enter TEAMWORK.

**Explosive Scenery Option, Multiplayer**
Enter BOOM. This option is in the Enviro-Mods menu.

**All Characters in Multiplayer**
Enter PARTY.

**Play as Bond Tux, Multiplayer**
Enter BLACKTIE.

**Play as Drake Suit, Multiplayer**
Enter NUMBER 1.

**Play as Bond Spacesuit, Multiplayer**
Enter ZERO G.

**Play as Goldfinger, Multiplayer**
Enter MIDAS.

**Play as Renard, Multiplayer**
Enter HEADCASE.

**Play as Scaramanga, Multiplayer**
Enter ASSASSIN.

**Play as Christmas Jones, Multiplayer**
Enter NUCLEAR.

**Play as Wai Lin, Multiplayer**
Enter MARTIAL.

**Play as Xenia Onatopp, Multiplayer**
Enter JANUS.

**Play as May Day, Multiplayer**
Enter BADGIRL.

**Play as Elektra King, Multiplayer**
Enter SLICK.

**Play as Jaws, Multiplayer**
Enter DENTAL.

**Play as Baron Samedi, Multiplayer**
Enter VOODOO.

**Play as Oddjob, Multiplayer**
Enter BOWLER.

**Play as Nick Nack, Multiplayer**

Enter BITESIZE.

**Play as Max Zorin, Multiplayer**

Enter BLIMP.

**Drive An SUV, Enemies Vanquished Level**

Start the Enemies Vanquished Level and pause the game. Hold L and press B, X, Y, B, Y, then release L.

**Race in Cobra, Enemies Vanquished Level**

Start the Enemies Vanquished Level and pause the game. Hold L and press X, X, B, B, Y, then release L.

Enter the following codes during the Paris Prelude, Enemies Vanquished, Island Infiltration, or Deep Descent levels:

**Faster Racing**

Pause the game, hold L and press B, Y, X, B, Y, X, then release L.

**Berserk Racing**

Pause the game, hold L and press B, Y, Y, B, Y, X, then release L.

**Trails**

Pause the game, hold L and press B, X, X, B, then release L.

**Double Armor**

Pause the game, hold L and press X, Y, B, X, X, then release L.

**Triple Armor**

Pause the game, hold L and press X, Y, B, X (x3), then release L.

**Quadruple Armor**

Pause the game, hold L and press X, Y, B, X (x4), then release L.

**Super Bullets**

Pause the game, hold L and press X (x4), then release L.

# LEGACY OF KAIN: BLOOD OMEN 2

**Begin with Soul Reaver and Iron Armor**

At the Main Menu press Z, R, L, B, X, Y.

# LORD OF THE RINGS: THE TWO TOWERS

### Health

Pause the game, hold L + R and press Y, Down, A, Up.

### Arrows

Pause the game, hold L + R and press A, Down, Y, Up.

### 1000 Upgrade Points

Pause the game, hold L + R and press A, Down (x3).

### Level 2 Skills

Pause the game, hold L + R and press X, Right, X, Right.

### Level 4 Skills

Pause the game, hold L + R and press Y, Up, Y, Up.

### Level 6 Skills

Pause the game, hold L + R and press B, Left, B, Left.

### Level 8 Skills

Pause the game, hold L + R and press A, A, Down, Down.

To access the following codes, you must first complete the game:

### Always Devastating

Pause the game, hold L + R and press B, B, X, X.

### Small Enemies

Pause the game, hold L + R and press Y, Y, A, A.

**All Upgrades**

Pause the game, hold L + R and press Y, X, Y, X.

**Invulnerable**

Pause the game, hold L + R and press Y, B, A, X.

**Slow Motion**

Pause the game, hold L + R and press Y, X, A, B.

**Unlimited Missile Weapons**

Pause the game, hold L + R and press B, X, A, Y.

# MAT HOFFMAN'S PRO BMX 2

**Level Select**

At the Title screen press B, Right, Right, Y, Down, B. This code works for Session, Free Ride, and Multiplayer modes.

**Boston, MA Level (Road Trip)**

At the Title screen press B, Up, Down, Down, Up, B.

**Chicago, IL Level (Road Trip)**

At the Title screen press B, Up, Y, Up, Y, B.

**Las Vegas, NV Level (Road Trip)**

At the Title screen press B, R, Left, L, Right, B.

**Los Angeles, CA Level (Road Trip)**

At the Title screen press B, Left, A, A, Left, B.

**New Orleans, LA Level (Road Trip)**

At the Title screen press B, Down, Right, Up, Left, B.

**Portland, OR Level (Road Trip)**

At the Title screen press Y, A, A, B, B, Y.

**Day Smith**

At the Title screen press Y, Up, Down, Up, Down, B.

**Vanessa**

At the Title screen press Y, Down, Left, Left, Down, B.

**Big Foot**

At the Title screen press Y, Right, Up, Right, Up, B.

**The Mime**

At the Title screen press Y, Left, Right, Left, Right, A.

### Volcano
At the Title screen press Y, Up, Up, A, Up, Up, Y.

### Street Bike
At the Title screen press A, Left, Left, L, R, Left.

### Bling 540 Bike
At the Title screen press A, R, Left, Left, R, Left.

### Second Costume
At the Title screen press X, L, Down, Up, R.

### Elvis Costume
At the Title screen press Y, L, L, Up, Up.

### BMX Costume
At the Title screen press Y, X, Left, Right, Left, X.

### Tiki Battle Mode
At the Title screen press L, L, Down, Right, X, L.

### Mat Hoffman Videos
At the Title screen press R, Left, Y, Left, Y, Left, R.

### Joe Kowalski Videos
At the Title screen press R, Up, Y, X, Down, R.

### Rick Thorne Videos
At the Title screen press R, L, R, R, L, R.

### Mike Escamilla Videos
At the Title screen press R, Y, A, A, Y, A, A, R.

### Simon Tabron Videos
At the Title screen press L, Z, R, L, Z, R.

### Kevin Robinson Videos
At the Title screen press R, Y, X, Down, Up, R.

### Cory Nastazio Videos
At the Title screen press R, X, Y, Y, X (x3), R.

### Ruben Alcantara Videos
At the Title screen press R, Left, Right, Left, Right, Left, R.

### Seth Kimbrough Videos

At the Title screen press R, Up, Down, Y (x3), R.

### Nate Wessel Videos

At the Title screen press R, Down, B, Y, Down, B, Y, R.

### All Music

At the Title screen press L, Left, Left, Right, Right, Left, A.

### No Display

At the Title screen press Down, B, X, A, Y.

# MEDAL OF HONOR: FRONTLINE

Select Passwords from the Options menu and enter the following. You need to turn on many of these cheats at the Bonus screen.

**Silver Bullet Mode**
Enter SILVERSHOT.

**Bullet Shield**
Enter REFLECTOR.

**Mohton Torpedo**
Enter BIGBOOMER.

**Perfectionist**
Enter FLAWLESS.

**Achilles' Head**
Enter HEADSUP.

**Snipe-O-Rama Mode**
Enter SUPERSHOT.

**Rubber Grenade**
Enter BOUNCE.

**Men with Hats**
Enter MADHATTER.

**Invisible Enemies**
Enter HIDENSEEK.

**Mission Complete with Gold Star**
Enter SEAGULL.

**Mission 2: A Storm in the Port**
Enter EAGLE.

**Mission 3: Needle in a Haystack**
Enter HAWK.

**Mission 4: Several Bridges Too Far**
Enter PARROT.

**Mission 5: Rolling Thunder**
Enter DOVE.

**Mission 6: The Horten's Nest**
Enter TOUCAN.

# MEN IN BLACK 2: ALIEN ESCAPE

At the title screen, enter the following. These cheats may disable saves.

**Invincible**
Press Right, A, R, Y, Up, L, A, Left, L, B, A, R.

**All Weapons**
Press Up, Down, A, X, R, Y, Y, Left, B, L, L, Right.

**Level Select**
Press R, Y, Left, B, X, L, Left, Up, A, Down, L, X.

**Training Missions**
Press X, Up, L, Left, Y, A, R, B, Right, R, X, B.

**Boss Mode**
Press R, Y, Down, Down, A, L, Left, X, Right, Y, R, L.

**No Power-Up Drops**
Press Down, Up, A, X, Down, Up, A, X, L, L, X, B.

**Full Area Effect**
Press Left, A, Y, Up, A, Down, X, L, Left, R.

**Full Beam**
Press Left, B, Y, Right, L, X, Left, R, R, Y.

**Full Bolt**
Press Left, Right, Up, Down, L, B, Y, R, Left, Down, X, X.

**Full Homing**
Press Right, Up, X, L, Left, Left, L, Left, B, Left.

**Full Spread**
Press L, R, B, L, Down, Up, L, Right, Left, A.

**Agent Data**

Press Up, Down, B, R, Left, L, Right, A, R, X, Up, R.

**Alien Data**

Press X, L, B, L, Down, Y, R, Right, A, Left, R, Y.

**Making Of Video**

Press B, L, R, B, Y, Down, X, A, Right, L, A, Up.

# MINORITY REPORT

Select Cheats from the Special menu and enter the following:

**Invincibility**
Enter LRGARMS.

**Level Warp All**
Enter PASSKEY.

**Level Skip**
Enter QUITER.

**All Combos**
Enter NINJA.

**All Weapons**
Enter STRAPPED.

**Infinite Ammo**
Enter MRJUAREZ.

**Super Damage**
Enter SPINACH.

**Health**
Enter BUTTERUP.

Select Alternate Heroes from the Special menu to find the following codes:

**Clown Hero**
Enter SCARYCLOWN.

**Convict Hero**
Enter JAILBREAK.

**GI John Hero**
Enter GNRLINFANTRY.

**Lizard Hero**
Enter HISSSS.

**Moseley Hero**
Enter HAIRLOSS.

**Nara Hero**
Enter WEIGHTGAIN.

**Nikki Hero**
Enter BIGLIPS.

**Robot Hero**
Enter MRROBOTO.

**Super John Hero**
Enter SUPERJOHN.

**Zombie Hero**
Enter IAMSODEAD.

**Free Aim**
Enter FPSSTYLE.

**Pain Arenas**
Enter MAXIMUMHURT.

**Armor**
Enter STEELUP.

**Baseball Bat**
Enter SLUGGER.

**Rag Doll**
Enter CLUMSY.

**Bouncy Men**
Enter BOUNZMEN.

**Wreck the Joint**
Enter CLUTZ.

**Dramatic Finish**
Enter STYLIN.

**Ending**
Enter WIMP.

**Concept Art**
Enter SKETCHPAD.

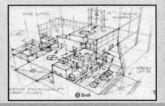

**All Movies**

Enter DIRECTOR.

**Do Not Select**

Enter DONOTSEL.

# MLB SLUGFEST 20-04

## Cheats

At the Match-Up screen, use B, Y, and X to enter the following codes, then press the appropriate direction. For example, for "Alien Team" (231 Down) press B two times, Y three times, X one time, then press Down.

| Code | Enter |
| --- | --- |
| Cheats Disabled | 111 Down |
| Unlimited Turbo | 444 Down |
| No Fatigue | 343 Up |
| No Contact Mode | 433 Left |
| 16' Softball | 242 Down |

| Code | Enter |
|------|-------|
| Rubber Ball | 242 Up |
| Whiffle Bat | 004 Right |
| Blade Bat | 002 Up |
| Bone Bat | 001 Up |
| Ice Bat | 003 Up |
| Log Bat | 004 Up |
| Mace Bat | 004 Left |
| Spike Bat | 005 Up |
| Big Head | 200 Right |
| Tiny Head | 200 Left |
| Max Batting | 300 Left |
| Max Power | 030 Left |
| Max Speed | 003 Left |
| Alien Team | 231 Down |
| Bobble Head Team | 133 Down |

| Casey Team | 233 Down |
|------------|----------|
| Dolphin Team | 102 Down |
| Dwarf Team | 103 Down |
| Eagle Team | 212 Right |
| Evil Clown Team | 211 Down |
| Gladiator Team | 113 Down |
| Horse Team | 211 Right |

| Code | Enter |
| --- | --- |
| Lion Team | 220 Right |
| Little League | 101 Down |
| Minotaur Team | 110 Down |
| Napalitano Team | 232 Down |

| | |
| --- | --- |
| Olshan Team | 222 Down |
| Pinto Team | 210 Right |
| Rivera Team | 222 Up |
| Rodeo Clown | 132 Down |
| Scorpion Team | 112 Down |
| Team Terry Fitzgerald | 333 Right |
| Team Todd McFarlane | 222 Right |
| Atlantis Stadium | 321 Left |
| Coliseum Stadium | 333 Up |

| | |
| --- | --- |
| Empire Park Stadium | 321 Right |
| Forbidden City Stadium | 333 Left |
| Midway Park Stadium | 321 Down |
| Monument Stadium | 333 Down |
| Rocket Park Stadium | 321 Up |
| Extended Time for Codes | 303 Up |

# NASCAR: DIRT TO DAYTONA

### $10,000

At the Main Menu, press Up, Down, Left, Right, Z, Left, Left.

# NBA 2K3

### Codes

Select Game Play from the Options menu, hold Left on the D-pad + Right on the Left Analog Stick and press START. Exit to the Options menu and the Codes option will appear.

### Sega Sports, Visual Concepts, and NBA 2K3 Teams

Enter MEGASTARS as a code.

### Street Trash

Enter SPRINGER as a code.

### Duotone Draw

Enter DUOTONE as a code.

# NBA LIVE 2003

Create a player with the following last names. These characters will be available as free agents.

### B-Rich

Enter DOLLABILLS.

### Busta Rhymes

Enter FLIPMODE.

### DJ Clue

Enter MIXTAPES.

### Ghetto Fabulous

Enter GHETTOFAB.

### Hot Karl

Enter CALIFORNIA.

### Just Blaze

Enter GOODBEATS.

# NBA STREET VOL. 2

Select Pick Up Game, hold L and enter the following when "Enter cheat codes now" appears at the bottom of the screen:

**Unlimited Turbo**
Press B, B, Y, Y.

**ABA Ball**
Press X, B, X, B.

**WNBA Ball**
Press X, Y, Y, X.

**No Display Bars**
Press B, X (x3).

**All Jerseys**
Press X, Y, B, B.

**All Courts**
Press B, Y, Y, B.

**St. Lunatics Team and All Street Legends**
Press X, Y, B, Y.

**All NBA Legends**
Press X, Y, Y, B.

**Classic Michael Jordan**
Press X, Y, X, X.

**Explosive Rims**
Press X (x3), Y.

**Small Players**
Press Y, Y, X, B.

**Big Heads**
Press X, B, B, X.

**No Counters**
Press Y, Y, X, X.

**Ball Trails**
Press Y, Y, Y, B.

**All Quicks**
Press Y, X, Y, B.

**Easy Shots**
Press Y, X, B, Y.

**Hard Shots**
Press Y, B, X, Y.

# OUTLAW GOLF

### All Characters and Clubs

Start a new game and enter **Golf_Gone_Wild** as a name.

### Larger Ball

During gameplay, hold L and press Up (x3), Down.

### Smaller Ball

During gameplay, hold L and press Down (x3), Up.

### No Wind

During gameplay, hold L and press Up, Left, Down, Right, Up, Left, Down, Right, X, X.

### Beating Token

During gameplay, hold L and press Z, X, Z, Z, X. This only works if you have used all of your tokens.

# RED FACTION II

Select Cheats from the Extras menu and enter the following:

### Unlock Everything

Enter B, B, A, A, Y, X, Y, X.

### All Cheats

Enter Y, X, B, X, Y, A, B, A.

### Level Select

Enter X, Y, A, B, Y, X, A, A.

### Super Health

Enter A, A, Y, B, Y, B, X.

## GameCube™                                          R

**Infinite Grenades**
Enter X, A, X, Y, A, X, A, X.

**Director's Cut**
Enter Y, A, X, B, X, A, Y, B.

**Rapid Rails**
Enter X, Y, X, Y, A, A, B, B.

**Extra Chunky**
Enter X, X, X, X, B, A, X, X.

**Infinite Ammo**
Enter Y, B, A, X, Y, X, A, B.

**Wacky Deaths**
Enter B, B, B, B, B, B, B, B.

**Walking Dead**
Enter A, A, A, A, A, A, A, A.

**Rain Of Fire Cheat**
Enter Y, Y, Y, Y, Y, Y, Y, Y.

**Gibby Explosions**
Enter B, X, A, Y, B, X, A, Y.

**Bouncing Grenades**
Enter X, X, X, X, X, X, X, X.

**Gibby Ammunition**
Enter A, A, A, A, X, Y, A, A.

**Joker Cheat**
Enter Y, A, Y, A, Y, A, Y, A.

## ROBOTECH: BATTLECRY

**Cheat Mode**

Select New Game or Load Game, hold L + R + Z and press Left, Up, Down, A, Right, B, START. After doing so, enter the following:

**Invincibility**
Enter SUPERMECH.

**Level Select**
Enter WEWILLWIN.

**All Multiplayer Levels**
Enter MULTIMAYHEM.

**All Models and Awards**
Enter WHERESMAX.

**Alternate Paint Schemes**
Enter MISSMACROSS.

**Gunpod Ammunition Refilled Faster**
Enter SPACEFOLD.

**Missiles Refilled Faster**
Enter MARSBASE.

**Gunpod and Missiles Refilled Faster**
Enter MIRIYA.

**One-Shot Kills**
Enter BACKSTABBER.

**One-Shot Kills, Sniper Mode**
Enter SNIPER.

**Upside Down**
Enter FLIPSIDE.

**Disable Codes**
Enter CLEAR.

# ROCKY

### Punch Double Damage

At the Main Menu, hold R and press Right, Down, Left, Up, Left, L.

### Double Speed Boxing

At the Main Menu, hold R and press Down, Left, Down, Up, Right, L.

### All Default Boxers and Arenas

At the Main Menu, hold R and press Right, Down, Up, Left, Up, L. This code *doesn't* unlock Mickey or the Rocky Statue.

### All Default Boxers, Arenas, and Rocky Statue

At the Main Menu, hold R and press Right (x3), Left, Right, L.

### All Default Boxers, Arenas, Rocky Statue, and Mickey

At the Main Menu, hold R and press Up, Down, Down, Left, Left, L.

### Full Stats, Tournament and Exhibition Modes

At the Main Menu, hold R and press Left, Up, Up, Down, Right, L.

### Full Stats, Movie Mode

At the Main Menu, hold R and press Right, Down, Down, Up, Left, L.

# SHOX

### $2,500,000

Start a new game in single player mode and enter **LOADED** as a name.

# SONIC MEGA COLLECTION

### Blue Sphere

Play Sonic 1 and Sonic 3D 20 times each.

### The Comix Zone

At the Manuals screen, press Z, Z, Z, Up, Up, Up, Down, Down, Down, L, R, Z.

### Flicky

Play Dr. Robotnik's Mean Bean Machine 20 times.

### Ristar

Play every game 20 times.

### Sonic 2 and Knuckles

Play Sonic 2 and Sonic Spinball 20 times each.

### Sonic 3 and Knuckles

Play Sonic 3 and Sonic and Knuckles 20 times each.

## SONIC THE HEDGEHOG

### Level Select

At the Title screen, press Up, Down, Left, Right.

### Debug Mode

At the Title screen, press Up, X, Down, X, Left, X, Right. Hold B, then hold START until level loads. Press A for Debug Mode.

## SONIC THE HEDGEHOG 2

### Level Select

Select Sound Test from the Options menu and play the following sounds in order: 19, 65, 9, and 17. Hold X and press START. At the Title screen, hold B and press START.

### Debug Mode

After enabling the Level Select code, use the Sound Test to play the following sounds in order: 1, 9, 9, 2, 1, 1, 2, 4. Select the desired level, then hold B + START until the level loads.

## SONIC THE HEDGEHOG 3

### Level Select

After the Sega logo fades and as Sonic appears, press Up, Up, Down, Down, Up (x4). At the Title screen, press Up to access the Level Select.

### Debug Mode

With the Level Select code enabled, hold B and press Start.

## SONIC SPINBALL

### Level Select

At the Options menu, press B, Down, A, Down, X, Down, B, A, Up, B, X, Up, A, X, Up.

## FLICKY

### Level Select

Start a game and hold Up + A + X + Start. When Round 1 appears, release the buttons.

## RISTAR

Enter the following as passwords:

| Password | Effect |
|----------|--------|
| ILOVEU | Level Select |
| MUSEUM | Bosses Only |
| SUPERB | Very Hard Difficulty |
| DOFEEL | Time Attack |
| MAGURO | Different Sounds |
| MIEMIE | Hidden Items |
| XXXXXX | Disable Codes |

# SPEED KINGS

Enter the following as your Handle:

### Complete Driving Test

Enter .TEST9.

### All Meets Won

Enter .MEET6.

### Respect Points

Enter .Resp ##. Replace ## with the desired amount of respect.

### Master Cheat

Enter borkbork as a name.

# STAR WARS BOUNTY HUNTER

Enter the following at the Code Setup screen:

### Chapter Codes

| Chapter | Code |
|---------|------|
| 1 | SEEHOWTHEYRUN |
| 2 | CITYPLANET |
| 3 | LOCKDOWN |
| 4 | DUGSOPLENTY |
| 5 | BANTHAPOODOO |
| 6 | MANDALORIANWAY |

## Level Codes

| Level | Code |
| --- | --- |
| 1 | BEAST PIT |
| 2 | GIMMEMYJETPACK |
| 3 | CONVEYORAMA |
| 4 | BIGCITYNIGHTS |
| 5 | IEATNERFMEAT |
| 6 | VOTE4TRELL |
| 7 | LOCKUP |
| 8 | WHAT A RIOT |
| 9 | SHAFTED |
| 10 | BIGMOSQUITOS |
| 11 | ONEDEADDUG |
| 12 | WISHIHADMYSHIP |
| 13 | MOS GAMOS |
| 14 | TUSKENS R US |
| 15 | BIG BAD DRAGON |
| 16 | MONTROSSISBAD |
| 17 | VOSAISBADDER |
| 18 | JANGOISBADDEST |

### All Concept Art

Enter R ARTISTS ROCK.

### All TGC Cards

Enter GO FISH.

# STAR WARS: THE CLONE WARS

Select Bonuses from the Options menu, then select Codes to enter the following:

### Invincibility

Enter IWITHFORCE as a password.

### All Missions

Enter GASMASK as a password.

### Play Ewok Freedom Song

Press Up, Up, Down, Down, Left, Right, Left, Right, B, A, START.

### Team Photos

Enter SAYCHEESE.

**Unlimited Ammo**
Enter CHOSEN1.

**Bonus Objectives**
Enter YUB YUB.

**All Cutscenes**
Enter CINEMA.

**All Multiplayer Maps**
Enter FRAGFIESTA.

**Battle Droid in Academy**
Enter ROGERROGER.

**Wookie in Academy**
Enter FUZZBALL.

# STAR WARS JEDI KNIGHT II: JEDI OUTCAST

Select Cheats from the Extras menu to enter the following codes:

**Level Select**
Enter DINGO.

**Lightsaber from Beginning**
Enter FUDGE.

**Infinite Health**
Enter BUBBLE.

**Inifinite Ammo**
Enter BISCUIT.

**All Movies**
Enter FLICKY.

**Multiplayer Characters**
Enter PEEPS.

**First Seven Levels**
Enter CHERRY.

**Demo Stage**
Enter DEMO.

# STREET HOOPS

Select Cheats from Game Settings and enter the following:

**Clown Uniforms**
Press R, Y, R, R.

**Block Party**
Press Y, R, L, Y.

**Cowboy Uniforms**
Press Y, Y, X, Y.

**Power Game**
Press R, L, L, Y.

**Elvis Uniforms**
Press Y, L, Y, R, Y, Y, X, Y.

**Black Ball**
Press L, R, L, L.

**Kung Fu Uniforms**
Press R, R, L, Y.

**And I Ball**
Press X, L, X, X, L, Y, R, L.

**Pimp Uniforms**
Press R, X, L, L.

**ABA Ball**
Press Y, Y, R, X.

**Tuxedo Uniforms**
Press Y, X, R, Y.

**Globe Ball**
Enter R, Y, R, R, L, X, Y, X.

**Tommy Tallarico Uniforms**
Press L (x3), R, Y, R, R, X.

**Normal Ball**
Press R, X, X, L.

**All Courts**
Press L, L, X, L, Y, R, R, X.

**$10,000,000**
Press R, Y, R, Y, L, L, X, Y.

**All Players**
Press Y, Y, R, L, Y, Y, X, Y.

# SUPERMAN: SHADOW OF APOKOLIPS

Select Cheat Codes from the Options menu to enter the following codes:

**Unlock Everything**
Enter I WANT IT ALL.

**Unlimited Health**
Enter FIRST AID.

**All Attack Mode Stages**
Enter SIGHTSEEING.

**Unlimited Superpower**
Enter JUICED UP.

**Empty Superpower**
Enter JOR EL.

**Disable Time Limits**
Enter STOP THE CLOCK.

**Slow Motion**
Enter SLOW MOTION.

**All Character Bios**
Enter INTERVIEW.

**All Movies**
Enter POPCORN.

**Explore Metropolis Mode**
Enter WANDERER.

**Shooting Gallery and Item Hunt Challenges (Explore Metropolis Mode)**
Enter CREEP.

**Easier Test of Strength Mode**
Enter SORE FINGER.

**Clark Kent**
Enter SECRET IDENTITY.

**Parasite**
Enter FEELING DRAINED.

**Extra Hard Difficulty**
Enter NAILS.

**Silent Movie Mode**
Enter RETRO.

**Reverse Controls**
Enter SUPERMAN.

## THE SIMPSONS: HIT & RUN

Select the Options from the main menu, hold L + R and enter the following:

**Red Brick Car**
Enter B, B, Y, X.

**Fast Cars**
Enter X, X, X, X.

**Faster Cars**
Enter Y, Y, Y, Y.

**One-Hit Wreck**
Enter Y, Y, X, X.

**Use Horn to Jump in Car**
Enter X, X, X, Y.

**Show Speed**

Enter Y, Y, B, X.

**Change Camera**

Enter B, B, B, A.

**Grid View**

Enter B, A, B, Y.

**Trippy**

Enter Y, B, Y, B.

**Credits Dialog**

Enter A, X, X, Y.

**Holiday Decorated Living Room**

Change the date of your system to Thanksgiving, Halloween or Christmas for a new look.

# THE SIMPSONS: ROAD RAGE

**New Year's Krusty**

At the Options screen, hold L + R and press B, B, X, Y. Or, set the GameCube date to January 1.

**Halloween Bart**

At the Options screen, hold L + R and press B, B, X, A. Or, set the GameCube date to October 31.

**Thanksgiving Marge**

At the Options screen, hold L + R and press B, B, X, X. Or, set the GameCube date to Thanksgiving.

**Christmas Apu**

At the Options screen, hold L + R and press B, B, X, B. Or, set the GameCube date to December 25.

**Flat Characters**

At the Options screen, hold L + R and press X (x4).

**No Map**

At the Options screen, hold L + R and press Y, B, B, X.

**Horizontal Split Screen, Multiplayer Mode**

At the Options screen, hold L + R and press Y (x4).

**Night**

At the Options screen, hold L + R and press A (x4).

**Alternate Camera Views**

At the Options screen, hold L + R and press B (x4).

**More Camera Options**

At the Options screen, hold L + R and press B, A (x3).

**Collision Lines**

At the Options screen, hold L + R and press B, B, A, A.

**Smithers in Mr. Burns's Limousine**

At the Options screen, hold L + R and press B, B, Y, Y.

**Nuclear Bus**

At the Options screen, hold L + R and press B, B, Y, A.

**Red Brick Car**

At the Options screen, hold L + R and press B, B, Y, X.

**Special Moves**

At the Options screen, hold LI + RI and press A, B, B, A.

Road Rage Roll, hold Gas + Brake + Handbrake in air

Speed Boost, hold Gas + Handbrake, then release Handbrake

**Time Trial**

At the Options screen, hold L + R and press X, B, Y, A.

**Slow Motion**

At the Options screen, hold L + R and press A, X, B, Y.

**Disable Codes**

At the Options screen, hold L + R and press START (x4).

# THE SIMS

At the Main Menu, press L + R to enter the following codes:

**Play The Sims Mode, All 2-Player Games, Objects, and Skins**

Enter MIDAS. Select Get A Life, and start a new game. Join Roxy in the hot tub, pause the game, and quit.

**All Objects Cost Zero Simoleans**

Enter FREEALL.

**Party Motel, 2-Player Game**

Enter PARTY M.

**Play The Sims Mode**

Enter SIMS.

# TIGER WOODS PGA TOUR 2004

**All Golfers and Courses**
Enter THEKITCHENSINK.

**All Golfers**
Enter CANYOUPICKONE

**All Courses**
Enter ALLTHETRACKS.

**Target Shootout**
Enter sherwood target.

**Ace Andrews**
Enter ACEINTHEHOLE.

**Cedric The Entertainer**
Enter CEDDYBEAR.

**Dominic "The Don" Donatello**
Enter DISCOKING.

**Downtown Brown**
Enter DTBROWN.

**Edwin "Pops" Masterson**
Enter EDDIE.

**Erica Ice**
Enter ICYONE.

**Hamish "Mulligan" McGregor**
Enter DWILBY.

**Moa "Big Mo" Ta'a Vatu**
Enter ERUPTION.

**Solita Lopez**
Enter SHORTGAME.

**Sunday Tiger**
Enter 4REDSHIRTS.

**Takeharu "Tsunami" Moto**
Enter EMERALDCHAMP.

**Val Summers**
Enter BEVERLYHILLS.

**"Yosh" Tanigawa**
Enter THENEWLEFTY.

# TONY HAWK'S PRO SKATER 4

Select Cheat Codes from the Options screen to enter the following codes:

## Unlock Everything

Enter WATCH_ME_XPLODE. Find the underscore in the Symbols section.

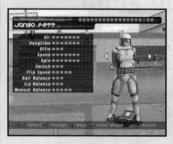

**Daisy**

Enter (o)(o).

**Always Special**

Enter G0LDEN.

**Perfect Manual**

Enter 2WHEELIN.

**Perfect Rail**

Enter BELIKEGEOFF.

**Matrix Mode**

Enter MRANDERSEN.

**Moon Gravity**

Enter GIANTSTEPS.

**Secret Created Skaters**

Create a new skater by entering the following names:

#$%@!
Aaron Skillman
Adam Lippmann
Andrew Skates
Andy Marchal
Angus
Atiba Jefferson
Ben Scott Pye
Big Tex
Brian Jennings
Captain Liberty
Chauwa Steel
Chris Peacock
ConMan

Danaconda
Dave Stohl
DDT
DeadEndRoad
Fritz
Gary Jesdanun
grjost
Henry Ji
Jason Uyeda
Jim Jagger
Joe Favazza
John Rosser
Jow
Kenzo
Kevin Mulhall
Kraken
Lindsey Hayes

Matt Mcpherson
Maya's Daddy
Meek West
Mike Day
Mike Lashever
Mike Ward
Mr. Brad
Nolan Nelson
Parking Guy
Peasus
Pete Day
Rick Thorne
Sik
Stacey D
Stacey Ytuarte
Team Chicken
Ted Barber
Todd Wahoske
Top Bloke
Wardcore
Zac Zig Drake

Lisa G Davies
Little Man
Marilena Rixfor
Mat Hoffman

# TY THE TASMANIAN TIGER

### Show Hidden Objects

During gameplay, press L, R, L, R, Y, Y, X, B, B, X, Z, Z.

### All Abilities

During gameplay, press L, R, L, R, Y, Y, B, B, Y, B..

**Technorangs**

During gameplay, press L, R, L, R, Y, Y, Y, B, Y, B

**Unlimited Life**

At the Main Menu, press L, R, L, R, Y, Y, Y, Y, X, X.

**Unlock Movies**

At the Main Menu, press L, R, L, R, Y, Y, A, A, Z, B, Z, B.

# V-RALLY 3

**Floating Cars**

Enter 210741974 MARTY as a name.

**Small Cars**

Enter 01041977 BIGJIM as a name.

**Smashed Cars**

Enter 25121975 PILOU as a name.

**Jelly Cars**

Enter 07121974 FERGUS as a name.

**Flat Cars**

Enter 21051975 PTITDAV as a name.

**Stretched Cars**

Enter Gonzales SPEEDY as a name.

**Small Cars & High-Pitched Commentary**

Enter PALACH as a last name with no first name.

# WRECKLESS

**Gold Rating on All Missions**

Highlight Unlimited Time, hold L + R + Right and press Z.

# WWE CRUSH HOUR

**All Vehicles and Level Select**

At the player select, press Y, Z, X, L.

**Kevin Nash**

At the player select, press L, X, Z, Y.

# X2: WOLVERINE'S REVENGE

### Level Select & All Challenges

At the Main Menu, press B, X, B, Y, B, X, L, R, Z.

### All Cerebro Files and Movies

At the Main Menu, press B, X, B, Y (x3), R, R, Z.

### All Costumes

At the Main Menu, press B, X, B, Y (x3), L, L, Z.

## Cheats

At the Main Menu, press B, B, X, X, Y, Y, X, X, L, L, R, R, Z. Pause the game to find the cheats.

# X-MEN: NEXT DIMENSION

## Quick Death Toggle

At the Main Menu, press Up, Up, Down, Down, X, Y, Y, X.

## Disable AI Toggle

At the Main Menu, press Up, Up, Down, Down, A, A, B, B, X, X, Y, Y.

## Unlimited Supers Toggle

At the Main Menu, press Up, Up, Down, Down, A, X, A, X.

# Games List

AGGRESSIVE INLINE . . . . . . . . . . . . . . . . . . . . . . . . . .230

BALLISTIC: ECKS VS. SEVER 2 . . . . . . . . . . . . . . . . . . .230

BRUCE LEE: RETURN OF THE LEGEND . . . . . . . . . .231

BUBBLE BOBBLE OLD AND NEW . . . . . . . . . . . . . .232

CAR BATTLER JOE . . . . . . . . . . . . . . . . . . . . . . . . . . .233

CASTLEVANIA: ARIA OF SORROW . . . . . . . . . . . . . .233

CT SPECIAL FORCES . . . . . . . . . . . . . . . . . . . . . . . . .233

DAREDEVIL: THE MAN WITHOUT FEAR . . . . . . . . . .234

DONKEY KONG COUNTRY . . . . . . . . . . . . . . . . . . .234

DOOM 2 . . . . . . . . . . . . . . . . . . . . . . . . . . . . . . . . . .234

DUAL BLADES . . . . . . . . . . . . . . . . . . . . . . . . . . . . . .235

FINDING NEMO . . . . . . . . . . . . . . . . . . . . . . . . . . . .235

FIRE PRO WRESTLING 2 . . . . . . . . . . . . . . . . . . . . . .235

GREMLINS . . . . . . . . . . . . . . . . . . . . . . . . . . . . . . . . .236

GT ADVANCE 3: PRO CONCEPT RACING . . . . . . .236

GUILTY GEAR X . . . . . . . . . . . . . . . . . . . . . . . . . . . . .237

ICE AGE . . . . . . . . . . . . . . . . . . . . . . . . . . . . . . . . . . .237

IRIDION II . . . . . . . . . . . . . . . . . . . . . . . . . . . . . . . . . .238

JAMES BOND 007: NIGHTFIRE . . . . . . . . . . . . . . . .239

JAZZ JACKRABBIT . . . . . . . . . . . . . . . . . . . . . . . . . . .239

JUSTICE LEAGUE: INJUSTICE FOR ALL . . . . . . . . . . .240

MATCHBOX CROSS TOWN HEROES . . . . . . . . . . . .240

MEDAL OF HONOR: UNDERGROUND . . . . . . . . . .241

MLB SLUGFEST 20-04 . . . . . . . . . . . . . . . . . . . . . . . .242

MORTAL KOMBAT: DEADLY ALLIANCE . . . . . . . . . .242

MUPPETS: ON WITH THE SHOW! . . . . . . . . . . . . . .242

MUPPET PINBALL MAYHEM . . . . . . . . . . . . . . . . . . .243

## GameBoy® Advance

ROBOT WARS: EXTREME DESTRUCTION . . . . . . . .243

SEGA SMASH PACK . . . . . . . . . . . . . . . . . . . . . . . .243

SPONGEBOB SQUAREPANTS: REVENGE OF THE
FLYING DUTCHMAN . . . . . . . . . . . . . . . . . . . . . . . .244

SPYHUNTER . . . . . . . . . . . . . . . . . . . . . . . . . . . . . .244

SPYRO: SEASON OF FLAME . . . . . . . . . . . . . . . . . .244

STAR WARS: JEDI POWER BATTLES . . . . . . . . . . . .246

STAR WARS EPISODE 2: THE NEW DROID ARMY . . .247

SUPER PUZZLE FIGHTER 2 TURBO . . . . . . . . . . . . .249

THE INCREDIBLE HULK . . . . . . . . . . . . . . . . . . . . .249

THE PINBALL OF THE DEAD . . . . . . . . . . . . . . . . . .249

THE SIMPSONS: ROAD RAGE . . . . . . . . . . . . . . . . .249

TOMB RAIDER: THE PROPHECY . . . . . . . . . . . . . . .250

URBAN YETI . . . . . . . . . . . . . . . . . . . . . . . . . . . . . .251

WILD THORNBERRYS: THE MOVIE . . . . . . . . . . . . .251

WOLFENSTEIN 3D . . . . . . . . . . . . . . . . . . . . . . . . .252

WORMS WORLD PARTY . . . . . . . . . . . . . . . . . . . . .252

X2: WOLVERINE'S REVENGE . . . . . . . . . . . . . . . . . .252

YU-GI-OH! THE ETERNAL DUELIST SOUL . . . . . . .253

YU-GI-OH! WORLDWIDE EDITION: STAIRWAY TO THE
DESTINED DUEL . . . . . . . . . . . . . . . . . . . . . . . . . . .253

## AGGRESSIVE INLINE

### All Skaters

At the Title screen, press L, L, B, B, R, R, L, R.

### Level Select

At the Title screen, press Up, Down, Up, Down, Left, Right, B, R.

# BALLISTIC: ECKS VS. SEVER 2

### Invincibility

Enter DEATHWISH as a password.

### Invisible

Enter DOYOUCME as a password.

### All Weapons

Enter TOOLEDUP as a password.

### Shotgun Rapid Fire

Enter MYBIGUN as a password.

### Unlimited Ammunition

Enter BIGPOCKET as a password.

### One-Shot Kills

Enter OOHSTOPIT as a password.

### Extra Damage on Explosion

Enter ACMEBANGS as a password.

### Motionless Enemies

Enter COLDFEET as a password.

### Alternate Sounds

Enter HORNBLOW as a password.

**Passwords**

| Level | Ecks | Sever |
|-------|------|-------|
| 2 | SMOKEY | RAVEN |
| 3 | BUTTERFLY | FIREFLY |
| 4 | COVEY | BULLDOG |
| 5 | TIGER | DRAGON |
| 6 | HORNET | LOUDMOUTH |
| 7 | LITTERBUG | STINGER |
| 8 | MUSTANG | NAIL |
| 9 | SPECTRE | ZORRO |
| 10 | NIMROD | XRAY |
| End | SPOOKY | REDDOG |

# BRUCE LEE: RETURN OF THE LEGEND

**Director's Cut**

Press Up, R, Select, R, Up, Select, Select.

**Time Challenge**

Press Up, Down, Up, R, Up, Down, Select.

**Gallery**

Press Down, Up, Down, R, R, Select, Left.

**Hai Feng is Invincible**

Press Down, Down, R, R, Up, Up, Select.

### Unlimited Ammunition

Press R, Up, R, Up, R, Up, R.

### Select Big Thugs

Press Right, Left, Right, Left, Right, Left, Right.

### Select Texases

Press Up, Down, Left, Right, Up, Down, Left.

### Select Jamals

Press Right (x7).

### Randomize all Enemies

Press Up, Right, Down, R, R, Select, Left.

### Bruce '73 Costume

Press Right, Down, Down, R, R, Select, Left.

### Dragon Costume

Press Right, Up, Down, R, Up, Select, Left.

### Gold Costume

Press Right, Up, Up, R, R, Select, Left.

# BUBBLE BOBBLE OLD AND NEW

### Bubble Bobble New: Super Mode

At the Bubble Bobble New title screen, press Right, R, Left, L, Select, R, Select, L.

### Bubble Bobble Old: Original Mode

At the Bubble Bobble Old title screen, press L, R, L, R, L, R, Right, SELECT.

### Bubble Bobble Old: Power-Up Mode

At the Bubble Bobble Old title screen, press Select, R, L, Left, Right, R, SELECT, Right.

### Bubble Bobble Old: Super Mode

At the Bubble Bobble Old title screen, press Left, R, Left, Select, Left, L, Left, Select.

## CAR BATTLER JOE

### Jim Joe Zero Car

In Battle League, enter TODOROKI as a password.

# CASTLEVANIA: ARIA OF SORROW

Enter the following codes as a name, then start a new game:

### Use No Souls

Enter NOSOUL.

### Use No Items

Enter NOUSE.

### Play as Julius Belmont

After defeating the game with a good ending, enter JULIUS.

# CT SPECIAL FORCES

### Level Passwords

| Level | Password |
| --- | --- |
| The Arid Desert | 1608 |
| The Hostile Jungle | 2111 |
| The Forbidden City | 1705 |

### Character Select Passwords

Enter the following passwords to select a character before the level.

| Level | Password |
|-------|----------|
| Snow Covered Mountains, Level 1 | 0202 |
| The Hostile Jungle | 2704 |
| The Forbidden City | 0108 |

# DAREDEVIL: THE MAN WITHOUT FEAR

### Unlock Everything

Enter the password 41TK1S6ZNGV.

# DONKEY KONG COUNTRY

### 50 Lives

At the game select, highlight Erase. Then hold Select and press B, A, R, R, A, L.

# DOOM 2

### God Mode

Press Start to pause game play, then hold L + R and press A, A, B, A (x5).

### Disable God Mode

Press Start to pause game play, then hold L + R and press A, A, B, A, B (x4).

### Computer Map

Press Start to pause game play, then hold L + R and press B, A (x7)

### Radiation Suit

Press Start to pause game play, then hold L + R and press B, B, A (x6)

### Invincibility

Press Start to pause game play, then hold L + R and press B (x3), A (x5)

### Berserk

Press Start to pause game play, then hold L + R and press B, A, B, A (x5)

### Weapons, Items, Keys

Press Start to pause game play, then hold L + R and press A, B, B, A (x5).

# DUAL BLADES

### Impossible Difficulty

At the Options screen, highlight Difficulty and press Left (x4), Right, Right, Left, Right, B.

# FINDING NEMO

### Level Select and Gallery

Enter the password M6HM.

### Passwords

| Level | Password |
|-------|----------|
| 2 | HZ51 |
| 3 | ZZ51 |
| 4 | 8061 |
| 5 | QHP1 |
| 6 | 8BP1 |
| 7 | 73P1 |
| 8 | 8MN2 |
| 9 | 7452 |

# FIRE PRO WRESTLING 2

### All Wrestlers

Edit a wrestler using the following information, then save the wrestler.

Nick Name: ALL

Last Name: WRESTLER

First Name: CLEAR

Exchange: Off

Middle: NONE

## GREMLINS

| Level | Password | Stripe Time Attack |
|-------|----------|--------------------|
| The Bank | GIZMO | CRUEL |
| The Police Station | BILLY | WATER |
| The Cinema | FUNNY | POWER |
| The Firehouse | TORCH | FLAME |
| The Final Encounter | GIFTS | MAGIC |

## GT ADVANCE 3: PRO CONCEPT RACING

### All Cars

At the Title screen, hold L + B and press Left.

### All Tracks

At the Title screen, hold L + B and press Right.

### All Tune Ups

At the Title screen, hold L + B and press Up.

### Extra Modes

At the Title screen, hold L + B and press Down.

# GUILTY GEAR X

### Extra Mode

At the main menu, press Right, Down, Left, R, R.

### Limit Release Mode

At the title screen, press L, R, A, A, A.

### Dizzy

At the title screen, press Down, Down, R, L, R.

### Testament

At the title screen, press Up, Down, Right, Left, A.

### GG Mode

At the title screen, press Left, Down, Right, L, L.

### Original Mode

At the title screen, press A, B, A, L, L.

# ICE AGE

### Level Select

Enter NTTTTT as a password.

### Art Gallery

Enter MFKRPH as a password.

### Level Passwords

| Level | Password |
|-------|----------|
| 2 | PBBQBB |
| 3 | QBCQBB |
| 4 | SBFQBB |
| 5 | DBKQBB |
| 6 | NBTQBB |

| Level | Password |
|-------|----------|
| 7 | PCTQBB |
| 8 | RFTQBB |
| 9 | CKTQBB |
| 10 | MTTQBB |

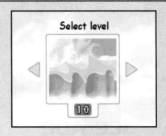

Select level

10

# IRIDION II

**Easy Passwords**

| Level | Password |
|-------|----------|
| 2 | SBJS5 |
| 3 | 9CRT5 |
| 4 | T3KG3 |
| 5 | 93PNV |
| 6 | 95FN3 |
| 7 | 5MYCX |
| 8 | 6C3L5 |
| 9 | PW3NX |
| 10 | 649QV |
| 11 | NFK2V |
| 12 | 5DS2V |
| 13 | !GDV5 |
| 14 | T7H8X |
| 15 | !9ROX |
| End | 4RC8! |

## JUKEBOX

Enter CH4LL as a password.

# JAMES BOND 007: NIGHTFIRE

### Level Select

Pause the game and press R, Left, L, Right, Up, Select, R.

### Unlimited Health

Pause the game and press R, Left, L, Right, Up, Select, Left.

### 500 Bullets

Pause the game and press R, Left, L, Right, Up, Select, Right.

### High-Pitched Voices

Pause the game and press R, Left, L, Right, Up, Select, L.

## JAZZ JACKRABBIT

### 500 Credits

Pause the game and press Right, Left, Right, Left, L, R, Up, Up, R, R, L, L.

### 1000 Credits

Pause the game and press Up, Down, Up, Down, Left, Right, L, R, L, R, R, L.

### 5000 Credits

Pause the game and press Up, Right, Down, Left, L, L, Right, Left, R, R, L, L.

# JUSTICE LEAGUE: INJUSTICE FOR ALL

### Invulnerability

Pause the game, highlight Resume and press SELECT, START.

# MATCHBOX CROSS TOWN HEROES

### Passwords

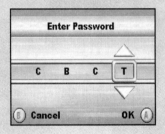

| Level | Password |
|-------|----------|
| 2 | CBCT |
| 3 | QBKL |
| 4 | CBCL |
| 5 | QBVJ |
| 6 | QBDJ |
| End | QBVN |

# MEDAL OF HONOR: UNDERGROUND

### Invulnerability

Enter MODEDEDIEU as a password.

### Passwords

| Level | Easy | Medium | Hard |
|-------|----------|----------|----------|
| 1 | TRILINGUE | IRRADIER | DOSSARD |
| 2 | SQUAME | FRIMAS | CUBIQUE |
| 3 | REVOLER | ESCARGOT | CHEMIN |
| 4 | FAUCON | DEVOIR | BLONDEUR |
| 5 | UNANIME | COALISER | BLESSER |
| 6 | ROULIS | BASQUE | AVOCAT |
| 7 | RELAVER | ROBUSTE | AFFINER |
| 8 | POUSSIN | SOYEUX | LAINE |
| 9 | PANOPLIE | TERRER | MESCLUN |
| 10 | NIMBER | VOULOIR | NORME |
| 11 | NIAIS | COUVERT | ORNER |
| 12 | KARMA | VOYANCE | PENNE |
| 13 | INCISER | PIGISTE | QUELQUE |
| 14 | GADOUE | NOMMER | REPOSE |
| 15 | FUSETTE | JETER | SALIFIER |
| 16 | EXCUSER | ENJAMBER | TROPIQUE |
| 17 | ENRICHIR | MORPHE | VOTATION |

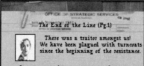

OFFICE OF STRATEGIC SERVICES

The End of the Line (Pg.1)

There was a traitor amongst us! We have been plagued with turncoats since the beginning of the resistance.

It enrages me how many men and woman are willing to sell their country and their soul for a few German Reichmarks.

No matter how carefully you screen the agents' backgrounds, a double agent always seems to sneak through the ranks.

# MLB SLUGFEST 20-04

### Cheats

Enter the following codes at the Matchup screen using the B, A and R buttons. For example, for All Fielders Run (132 Up), press B once, A three times and R twice, then press Up.

| Effect | Code |
| --- | --- |
| 1920 Mode | 242 Up |
| All Fielders Run | 132 Up |
| Backwards Fielders | 444 Right |
| Fireworks | 141 Right |
| Ghost Fielders | 313 Down |
| Nuke Ball | 343 Up |
| Skull Ball | 323 Left |

# MORTAL KOMBAT: DEADLY ALLIANCE

### 25,000 Koins

Enter KWIKKASH as your name.

# MUPPETS: ON WITH THE SHOW!

### All Mini-Games

Enter the password J09J4.

### Medium Difficulty

Enter the password G07n0.

### Hard Difficulty

Enter the password H08L2.

# MUPPET PINBALL MAYHEM

### Animal Machine

At the Options screen, select Credits. Then press Left, Right, Right, Up, R, Down, Down, L.

# ROBOT WARS: EXTREME DESTRUCTION

### Invincibility

Create a robot with the name HARD CASE.

### All Parts

Create a robot with the name SCRAP METAL.

### All Arenas

Create a robot with the name GLADIATOR.

# SEGA SMASH PACK

### Ecco The Dolphin

Pause the game with Ecco facing the screen and press Right, B, R, B, R, Down, R, Up. This unlocks Stage Select, Sound Select, and Unlimited Lives.

### Golden Axe

Select arcade mode and hold Down/Left + B and press Start at the Character Select screen. This unlocks Level Select.

### Golden Axe

Select arcade mode and hold Down/Left + A + R. Release the buttons and press Start to gain Nine Continues.

### Sonic Spinball

At the Options screen, press A, Down, B, Down, R, Down, A, B, Up, A, R, Up, B, R, Up. This unlocks Level Select. The following commands will start you at that level.

| Level | Command |
| --- | --- |
| 2 Lava Powerhouse | Hold A and press START |
| 3 The Machine | Hold B and press START |
| 4 Showdown | Hold R and press START |

### Sonic Spinball

At the Options screen, press A, Up, R, Up, L, Up, A, R, Down, A, L, Down, R, L, Down. This unlocks the game's Credits.

# SPONGEBOB SQUAREPANTS: REVENGE OF THE FLYING DUTCHMAN

### Debug Mode

Enter the password D3BVG-M0D3.

# SPYHUNTER

### Cheat List

You will need all of the save slots to do this cheat. At the copyright screen, press Left, Left, Right, R, R to clear the saves. Name the saves in order as follows:

BEST
GAME
EVER

You can now delete the second and third saves. Name these saves as follows for the indicated cheat:

| Cheat | Save Game Name |
| --- | --- |
| Arcade Level | EDACRA |
| All Alternate Vehicles | G6155 |
| Invincible/Infinite Ammo | SUPERSPY |

# SPYRO: SEASON OF FLAME

### Blue Spyro

At the Title screen, press Up, Up, Up, Up, Down, Left, Right, Down, B.

## All Portals

At the Title screen, press Up, Left, Up, Right, Up, Down, Up, Down, B.

Celestial Plains

## All Worlds in Atlas

At the Title screen, press Left, Right, Up, Up, Right, Left, Right, Up, B.

Realm Index
Sunny Plains
2/2500    0/37
Celestial Plains
0/3000    0/36
Starry Plains
0/2500    0/27

## Atlas Warping

At the Title screen, press Down, Up, Left, Left, Up, Left, Left, Right, B.**Infinite**

Ripto's Mondo Volcano
0/400    0/1
Complete:  0.0%

## Lives

At the Title screen, press Left, Right, Left, Right (x3), Up, Down, B.

## Infinite Shield for Agent 9

At the Title screen, press Left, Down, Up, Right, Left, Up, Up, Left, B.

## Inifinite Ammo

At the Title screen, press Right, Left, Up, Down, Right, Down, Up, Right, B.

## Never Drown

At the Title screen, press Down, Up, Right, Left, Right, Up, Right, Left, B.

## All Breath Types

At the Title screen, press Right, Down, Up, Right, Left, Up, Right, Down, B.

## Super Charge

At the Title screen, press Left, Left, Down, Up, Up, Right, Left, Left, B.

## Dragon Draughts Mini-Game

At the Title screen, press Right, Up, Down, Down, Down, Right, Up, Down, B.

# STAR WARS: JEDI POWER BATTLES

## Darth Maul Passwords

| Level | Password |
|-------|----------|
| 2 | VCJ0D2J |
| 3 | VCJ0G*J |
| 4 | VCJ0JKK |
| 5 | VCJ0LTK |
| 6 | VCJ0N2K |
| 7 | VCJ0Q1K |
| 8 | VCJ0SFK |
| 9 | VCJ0VPK |
| 10 | VCJ0XYK |

## Mace Windu Passwords

| Level | Password |
|-------|----------|
| 8 | VC1FCFH |
| 9 | VCJGCPH |
| 10 | VC1GCYH |

## Obi-Wan Passwords

| Level | Password |
|-------|----------|
| 2 | WDJ3B6F |
| 3 | XDJ3BFG |
| 4 | FDJ3BFG |
| 5 | GBJ3BPF |
| 6 | 0BJ3B6F |
| 7 | 1FJ3BYH |
| 8 | 2FJ3B6H |
| 9 | 3FJ3BFJ |
| 10 | 4FJ3BPJ |

# STAR WARS EPISODE 2: THE NEW DROID ARMY

After correctly entering the following passwords, you should receive an Invalid Password message.

## Level Select

Enter 2D4 as a password. Use L and R to select a level.

## 200 Health and 200 Force

Enter 8!T as a password.

## All Force Abilities

Enter FRC as a password.

## Luke Skywalker

Enter SKY as a password.

## Overhead Map

Enter CQL as a password.

## Change Controls

Enter BTW as a password.

## Disable Shadow

Enter !B4 as a password.

## Black Shadows

Enter SK8 as a password.

## Reduce Resolution

Enter GFX as a password.

## Toggle Language Option

Enter LNG as a password. Select Language from the Options screen.

## Passwords

After correctly entering the following passwords, you should receive a password accepted message.

| Level | Password |
| --- | --- |
| Droids at Speeder | D31 |
| Mos Espa | QK1 |
| Xelric Draw | BKT |
| Womp Rat Cave | FKW |
| Xelric Draw | C3P |
| Xelric Draw | CYD |
| Mos Espa | AK? |
| Hutt's Assassins | A3W |
| Mos Espa | AY4 |
| Dune Sea | KK4 |
| Moisture Farms | M34 |
| Moisture Farms | MYW |
| Jundland Wastes | TKP |
| Jundland Wastes | T3H |
| Jundland Wastes | TYQ |
| Jabba's Dungeon | J38 |
| Jabba's Dungeon | JY1 |
| Jabba's Dungeon | J?T |
| Jabba's Dungeon | J7J |
| High City | 7KQ |
| High City | 73D |
| High City (Interior) | 7YP |
| High City (Interior) | 7?W |
| Underlevels | !3C |
| Underlevels | !YL |
| Bentho's Nightclub | H3D |
| Core Bay | 6K7 |
| Core Bay | 63L |
| Jedi Temple | 532 |
| Jedi Archives | 4KX |
| Jedi Archives | 438 |
| Droid Factory Outskirts | XK1 |
| Production Facility 1 | 23X |
| Production Facility 1 | 2Y7 |
| Production Facility 2 | 3K2 |
| Production Facility 2 | 334 |
| Cortosis Processing Plant | WKP |

| Level | Password |
|-------|----------|
| Dual Duel! | W3H |
| Dual Duel! | WYQ |
| Droid Factory Core | ?KH |
| Droid Factory Core | ?3P |
| Duel with Vandalor | 8K7 |
| Race the Bombs | 831 |
| Ending | Y3W |

# SUPER PUZZLE FIGHTER 2 TURBO

The following codes work in Arcade, Vs. or Master Arcade modes.

### Akuma

At the Character Select screen, press L + B.

### Dan

At the Character Select screen, press L + R + B.

### Devilot

At the Character Select screen, press R + B.

# THE INCREDIBLE HULK

### Stage Skip

Pause the game and press Down, Right, Down, Right, Left, Left, Left, Up.

# THE PINBALL OF THE DEAD

### Boss Mode

Enter D0NTN33DM0N3Y as a password.

# THE SIMPSONS: ROAD RAGE

Enter the following as a password:

### All Cars, Levels and Bonuses

Enter Maggie, Willy, Bart, Chief Wiggum, Apu, Moe, Krusty, Barney.

### All Characters

Enter Bart, Bart, Lisa, Lisa, Marge, Marge, Barney, Barney.

# TOMB RAIDER: THE PROPHECY

### Credits

Enter ARIA as a password.

### Passwords

| Level | Password |
|-------|----------|
| 1 | PRLD |
| 2 | GAZE |
| 3 | MEDI |
| 4 | HAXE |
| 5 | PATH |
| 6 | BONE |
| 7 | TREE |
| 8 | LINK |
| 9 | KURZ |
| 10 | HELL |
| 11 | WEFX |
| 12 | MEMO |
| 13 | HEAR |
| 14 | FITZ |
| 15 | ELRC |
| 16 | CLIK |
| 17 | MGSL |

| Level | Password |
|-------|----------|
| 18 | ROMA |
| 19 | MONK |
| 20 | AEON |
| 21 | TIME |
| 22 | OLIM |
| 23 | LAND |
| 24 | DART |
| 25 | HILL |
| 26 | CHEX |
| 27 | STLK |
| 28 | MECH |
| 29 | ARKD |
| 30 | MUSH |
| 31 | LITH |

# URBAN YETI

### Unlock Everything

Select Continue and enter TONYGOLD.

# WILD THORNBERRYS: THE MOVIE

### Level Select

Enter HB5F as a password.

# WOLFENSTEIN 3D

## God Mode

Pause the game, hold L + R, and press A, A, B, A (x5).

## All Weapons, All Keys, Full Ammo, and Full Health

Pause the game, hold L + R, and press A, B, B, A (x5).

## Level Skip

Pause the game, hold L + R, and press A, B, A, A, B, B, B, A.

## Skip to Boss

Pause the game, hold L + R, and press A, B, A, A, B, B, A, A.

# WORMS WORLD PARTY

## All Weapons

During gameplay, open the Weapon Select menu. Highlight Skip Go and press A. Return to the Weapon Select screen, hold L + Down + B, and press SELECT (x4).

# X2: WOLVERINE'S REVENGE

## Alternate Costumes

At the Main Menu press Up, Down, Up, Down, Left, Right, Left, Right, B, A.

# YU-GI-OH! THE ETERNAL DUELIST SOUL
# YU-GI-OH! WORLDWIDE EDITION: STAIRWAY TO THE DESTINED DUEL

The following passwords work for both games:.

## Passwords

| Card | Password |
| --- | --- |
| 7 Colored Fish | 23771716 |
| 7 Completed | 86198326 |
| Acid Crawler | 77568553 |
| Acid Trap Hole | 41356845 |
| Air Eater | 08353769 |
| Air Marmot of Nefariousness | 75889523 |
| Akakieisu | 38035986 |
| Akihiron | 36904469 |
| Alligator's Sword | 64428736 |
| Alligator's Sword Dragon | 03366982 |
| Alpha The Magnet Warrior | 99785935 |
| Amazon of the Seas | 17968114 |
| Ameba | 95174353 |
| Amphibious Bugroth | 40173854 |
| Ancient Brain | 42431843 |
| Ancient Elf | 93221206 |
| Ancient Jar | 81492226 |
| Ancient Lizard Warrior | 43230671 |
| Ancient One of the Deep Forest | 14015067 |

| Card | Password |
|------|----------|
| Ancient Telescope | 17092736 |
| Ancient Tool | 49587396 |
| Ansatsu | 48365709 |
| Anthrosaurus | 89904598 |
| Anti Raigeki | 42364257 |
| Anti-Magic Fragrance | 58921041 |
| Appropriate | 48539234 |
| Aqua Chorus | 95132338 |
| Aqua Dragon | 86164529 |
| Aqua Madoor | 85639257 |
| Arlownay | 14708569 |
| Arma Knight | 36151751 |
| Armaill | 53153481 |
| Armed Ninja | 09076207 |
| Armored Glass | 36868108 |
| Armored Lizard | 15480588 |
| Armored Rat | 16246527 |
| Armored Starfish | 17535588 |
| Armored Zombie | 20277860 |
| Axe of Despair | 40619825 |
| Axe Raider | 48305365 |
| Baby Dragon | 88819587 |
| Backup Soldier | 36280194 |
| Banisher of the Light | 61528025 |
| Barox | 06840573 |
| Barrel Dragon | 81480460 |
| Barrel Lily | 67841515 |
| Barrel Rock | 10476868 |
| Basic Insect | 89091579 |
| Battle Ox | 05053103 |
| Battle Steer | 18246479 |
| Battle Warrior | 55550921 |
| Bean Soldier | 84990171 |
| Beast Fangs | 46009906 |
| Beastking of the Swamps | 99426834 |
| Beautiful Headhuntress | 16899564 |
| Beaver Warrior | 32452818 |
| Behegon | 94022093 |
| Bell of Destruction | 83555666 |
| Beta The Magnet Warrior | 39256679 |
| Bickuribox | 25655502 |

| Card | Password |
|------|----------|
| Big Eye | 16768387 |
| Big Insect | 53606874 |
| Big Shield Gardna | 65240384 |
| Binding Chain | 08058240 |
| Bio Plant | 07670542 |
| Black Dragon Jungle King | 89832901 |
| Black Illusion Ritual | 41426869 |
| Black Pendant | 65169794 |
| Blackland Fire Dragon | 87564352 |
| Bladefly | 28470714 |
| Blast Juggler | 70138455 |
| Blast Sphere | 26302522 |
| Block Attack | 25880422 |
| Blue Medicine | 20871001 |
| Blue-Eyed Silver Zombie | 35282433 |
| Blue-Eyes Toon Dragon | 53183600 |
| Blue-Eyes White Dragon | 89631139 |
| Blue-Eyes White Dragon | 80906030 |
| Blue-Winged Crown | 41396436 |
| Boar Soldier | 21340051 |
| Bolt Escargot | 12146024 |
| Book of Secret Arts | 91595718 |
| Bottom Dweller | 81386177 |
| Bracchio-Raidus | 16507828 |
| Breath of Light | 20101223 |
| Bright Castle | 82878489 |
| Burglar | 06297941 |
| Burning Spear | 18937875 |
| Buster Blader | 78193831 |
| Call of the Dark | 78637313 |
| Call of the Grave | 16970158 |
| Call Of The Haunted | 97077563 |
| Candle of Fate | 47695416 |
| Cannon Soldier | 11384280 |
| Castle of Dark Illusions | 00062121 |
| Castle Walls | 44209392 |
| Catapult Turtle | 95727991 |
| Ceasefire | 36468556 |
| Celtic Guardian | 91152256 |
| Ceremonial Bell | 20228463 |
| Chain Destruction | 01248895 |

| Card | Password |
|------|----------|
| Chain Energy | 79323590 |
| Change of Heart | 04031928 |
| Charubin the Fire Knight | 37421579 |
| Chorus of Sanctuary | 81380218 |
| Claw Reacher | 41218256 |
| Clown Zombie | 92667214 |
| Cockroach Knight | 33413638 |
| Confiscation | 17375316 |
| Crass Clown | 93889755 |
| Crawling Dragon | 67494157 |
| Crawling Dragon #2 | 38289717 |
| Crazy Fish | 53713014 |
| Crimson Sunbird | 46696593 |
| Crow Goblin | 77998771 |
| Crush Card | 57728570 |
| Curse of Dragon | 28279543 |
| Curse of Fiend | 12470447 |
| Curtain of the Dark Ones | 22026707 |
| Cyber Commander | 06400512 |
| Cyber Falcon | 30655537 |
| Cyber Jar | 34124316 |
| Cyber Saurus | 89112729 |
| Cyber Shield | 63224564 |
| Cyber Soldier | 44865098 |
| Cyber-Stein | 69015963 |
| Cyber-Tech Alligator | 48766543 |
| Dancing Elf | 59983499 |
| Dark Artist | 72520073 |
| Dark Assailant | 41949033 |
| Dark Chimera | 32344688 |
| Dark Elf | 21417692 |
| Dark Energy | 04614116 |
| Dark Gray | 09159938 |
| Dark Hole | 53129443 |
| D. Human | 81057959 |
| Dark King of the Abyss | 53375573 |
| Dark Magician | 46986414 |
| Dark Rabbit | 99261403 |
| Dark Sage | 92377303 |
| Dark Shade | 40196604 |
| Dark Witch | 35565537 |

| Card | Password |
| --- | --- |
| Dark Zebra | 59784896 |
| Dark-Eyes Illusionist | 38247752 |
| Darkfire Dragon | 17881964 |
| Darkfire Soldier #1 | 05388481 |
| Darkfire Soldier #2 | 78861134 |
| Darkness Approaches | 80168720 |
| Dark-Piercing Light | 45895206 |
| Darkworld Thorns | 43500484 |
| Deepsea Shark | 28593363 |
| Delinquent Duo | 44763025 |
| De-Spell | 19159413 |
| Destroyer Golem | 73481154 |
| Dice Armadillo | 69893315 |
| Dimensional Warrior | 37043180 |
| Disk Magician | 76446915 |
| Dissolverock | 40826495 |
| DNA Surgery | 74701381 |
| Dokuroizo the Grim Reaper | 25882881 |
| Doma The Angel of Silence | 16972957 |
| Doron | 00756652 |
| Dorover | 24194033 |
| Dragon Capture Jar | 50045299 |
| Dragon Piper | 55763552 |
| Dragon Seeker | 28563545 |
| Dragon Treasure | 01435851 |
| Dragon Zombie | 66672569 |
| Dragoness the Wicked Knight | 70681994 |
| Dream Clown | 13215230 |
| Driving Snow | 00473469 |
| Drooling Lizard | 16353197 |
| Dryad | 84916669 |
| Dunames Dark Witch | 12493482 |
| Dungeon Worm | 51228280 |
| Dust Tornado | 60082869 |
| Earthshaker | 60866277 |
| Eatgaboon | 42578427 |
| Eldeen | 06367785 |
| Electric Lizard | 55875323 |
| Electric Snake | 11324436 |
| Electro-Whip | 37820550 |
| Elegant Egotist | 90219263 |

| Card | Password |
|------|----------|
| Elf's Light | 39897277 |
| Empress Judge | 15237615 |
| Enchanted Javelin | 96355986 |
| Enchanting Mermaid | 75376965 |
| Eradicating Aerosol | 94716515 |
| Eternal Draught | 56606928 |
| Eternal Rest | 95051344 |
| Exchange | 05556668 |
| Exile of the Wicked | 26725158 |
| Exodia the Forbidden One | 33396948 |
| Eyearmor | 64511793 |
| Fairy Dragon | 20315854 |
| Fairy's Hand Mirror | 17653779 |
| Fairywitch | 37160778 |
| Faith Bird | 75582395 |
| Fake Trap | 03027001 |
| Feral Imp | 41392891 |
| Fiend Kraken | 77456781 |
| Fiend Reflection #1 | 68870276 |
| Fiend Reflection #2 | 02863439 |
| Fiend Sword | 22855882 |
| Fiend's Hand | 52800428 |
| Final Flame | 73134081 |
| Fire Kraken | 46534755 |
| Fire Reaper | 53581214 |
| Firegrass | 53293545 |
| Fireyarou | 71407486 |
| Fissure | 66788016 |
| Flame Cerebrus | 60862676 |
| Flame Champion | 42599677 |
| Flame Ghost | 58528964 |
| Flame Manipulator | 34460851 |
| Flame Swordsman | 45231177 |
| Flame Viper | 02830619 |
| Flash Assailant | 96890582 |
| Flower Wolf | 95952802 |
| Flying Kamakiri #1 | 84834865 |
| Flying Kamakiri #2 | 03134241 |
| Follow Wind | 98252586 |
| Forced Requisition | 74923978 |
| Forest | 87430998 |

| Card | Password |
|------|----------|
| Frenzied Panda | 98818516 |
| Fusion Sage | 26902560 |
| Fusionist | 01641882 |
| Gaia Power | 56594520 |
| Gaia the Dragon Champion | 66889139 |
| Gaia The Fierce Knight | 06368038 |
| Gale Dogra | 16229315 |
| Gamma the Magnet Warrior | 11549357 |
| Ganigumo | 34536276 |
| Garma Sword | 90844184 |
| Garma Sword Oath | 78577570 |
| Garnecia Elefantis | 49888191 |
| Garoozis | 14977074 |
| Garvas | 69780745 |
| Gatekeeper | 19737320 |
| Gazelle the King of Mythical Beasts | 05818798 |
| Gemini Elf | 69140098 |
| Genin | 49370026 |
| Germ Infection | 24668830 |
| Ghoul with an Appetite | 95265975 |
| Giant Flea | 41762634 |
| Giant Germ | 95178994 |
| Giant Mech-Soldier | 72299832 |
| Giant Rat | 97017120 |
| Giant Red Seasnake | 58831685 |
| Giant Scorpion of the Tundra | 41403766 |
| Giant Soldier of Stone | 13039848 |
| Giant Trunade | 42703248 |
| Giant Turtle Who Feeds on Flames | 96981563 |
| Gift of The Mystical Elf | 98299011 |
| Giganto | 33621868 |
| Giga-tech Wolf | 08471389 |
| Giltia the D. Knight | 51828629 |
| Goblin Fan | 04149689 |
| Goblin's Secret Remedy | 11868825 |
| Goddess of Whim | 67959180 |
| Goddess with the Third Eye | 53493204 |
| Gokibore | 15367030 |
| Graceful Charity | 79571449 |
| Graceful Dice | 74137509 |
| Grappler | 02906250 |

| Card | Password |
|------|----------|
| Gravedigger Ghoul | 82542267 |
| Gravekeeper's Servant | 16762927 |
| Graverobber | 61705417 |
| Graveyard and the Hand of Invitation | 27094595 |
| Great Bill | 55691901 |
| Great Mammoth of Goldfine | 54622031 |
| Great White | 13429800 |
| Green Phantom King | 22910685 |
| Greenkappa | 61831093 |
| Griffore | 53829412 |
| Griggle | 95744531 |
| Ground Attacker Bugroth | 58314394 |
| Gruesome Goo | 65623423 |
| Gryphon Wing | 55608151 |
| Guardian of the Labyrinth | 89272878 |
| Guardian of the Sea | 85448931 |
| Guardian of the Throne Room | 47879985 |
| Gust | 73079365 |
| Gust Fan | 55321970 |
| Gyakutenno Megami | 31122090 |
| Hane-Hane | 07089711 |
| Haniwa | 84285623 |
| Happy Lover | 99030164 |
| Hard Armor | 20060230 |
| Harpie Lady | 76812113 |
| Harpie Lady Sisters | 12206212 |
| Harpie's Brother | 30532390 |
| Harpie's Feather Duster | 18144506 |
| Harpie's Pet Dragon | 52040216 |
| Heavy Storm | 19613556 |
| Hercules Beetle | 52584282 |
| Hero of the East | 89987208 |
| Hibikime | 64501875 |
| High Tide Gyojin | 54579801 |
| Hinotama | 46130346 |
| Hinotama Soul | 96851799 |
| Hiro's Shadow Scout | 81863068 |
| Hitodenchak | 46718686 |
| Hitotsu-Me Giant | 76184692 |
| Holograh | 10859908 |
| Horn Imp | 69669405 |

| Card | Password |
|------|----------|
| Horn of Heaven | 98069388 |
| Horn of Light | 38552107 |
| Horn of the Unicorn | 64047146 |
| Hoshiningen | 67629977 |
| Hourglass of Courage | 43530283 |
| Hourglass of Life | 08783685 |
| House of Adhesive Tape | 15083728 |
| Hunter Spider | 80141480 |
| Hyo | 38982356 |
| Hyosube | 02118022 |
| Hyozanryu | 62397231 |
| Ice Water | 20848593 |
| Ill Witch | 81686058 |
| Illusionist Faceless Mage | 28546905 |
| Imperial Order | 61740673 |
| Insect Armor with Laser Cannon | 03492538 |
| Insect Queen | 91512835 |
| Insect Soldiers of the Sky | 07019529 |
| Inspection | 16227556 |
| Invader from Another Dimension | 28450915 |
| Invader of the Throne | 03056267 |
| Invigoration | 98374133 |
| Jellyfish | 14851496 |
| Jigen Bakudan | 90020065 |
| Jinzo | 77585513 |
| Jinzo #7 | 32809211 |
| Jirai Gumo | 94773007 |
| Judge Man | 30113682 |
| Just Desserts | 24068492 |
| Kagemusha of the Blue Flame | 15401633 |
| Kageningen | 80600490 |
| Kairyu-Shin | 76634149 |
| Kaiser Dragon | 94566432 |
| Kamakiriman | 68928540 |
| Kaminari Attack | 09653271 |
| Kaminarikozou | 15510988 |
| Kamionwizard | 41544074 |
| Kanikabuto | 84103702 |
| Karate Man | 23289281 |
| Karbonala Warrior | 54541900 |
| Kattapillar | 81179446 |

| Card | Password |
| --- | --- |
| Key Mace #2 | 20541432 |
| Killer Needle | 88979991 |
| King Fog | 84686841 |
| King of Yamimakai | 69455834 |
| Kiseitai | 04266839 |
| Kojikocy | 01184620 |
| Kotodama | 19406822 |
| Koumori Dragon | 67724379 |
| Krokodilus | 76512652 |
| Kumootoko | 56283725 |
| Kunai with Chain | 37390589 |
| Kurama | 85705804 |
| Kuriboh | 40640057 |
| Kwagar Hercules | 95144193 |
| La Jinn the Mystical Genie of the Lamp | 97590747 |
| Labyrinth Tank | 99551425 |
| Lady of Faith | 17358176 |
| LaLa Li-oon | 09430387 |
| Larvae | 94675535 |
| Laser Cannon Armor | 77007920 |
| Last Day of Witch | 90330453 |
| Last Will | 85602018 |
| Laughing Flower | 42591472 |
| Launcher Spider | 87322377 |
| Lava Battleguard | 20394040 |
| Left Arm of the Forbidden One | 07902349 |
| Left Leg of the Forbidden One | 44519536 |
| Legendary Sword | 61854111 |
| Leghul | 12472242 |
| Leogun | 10538007 |
| Lesser Dragon | 55444629 |
| Light of Intervention | 62867251 |
| Lightforce Sword | 49587034 |
| Liquid Beast | 93108297 |
| Little Chimera | 68658728 |
| Little D | 42625254 |
| Lord of D | 17985575 |
| Lord of the Lamp | 99510761 |
| Lord of Zemia | 81618817 |
| Luminous Spark | 81777047 |
| Lunar Queen Elzaim | 62210247 |

| Card | Password |
|------|----------|
| Mabarrel | 98795934 |
| Machine Conversion Factory | 25769732 |
| Machine King | 46700124 |
| Magic Jammer | 77414722 |
| Magic Thorn | 53119267 |
| Magical Ghost | 46474915 |
| Magical Hats | 81210420 |
| Magical Labyrinth | 64389297 |
| Magic-Arm Shield | 96008713 |
| Magician of Faith | 31560081 |
| Maha Vailo | 93013676 |
| Maiden of the Moonlight | 79629370 |
| Major Riot | 09074847 |
| Malevolent Nuzzler | 99597615 |
| Mammoth Graveyard | 40374923 |
| Man Eater | 93553943 |
| Man-Eater Bug | 54652250 |
| Man-Eating Black Shark | 80727036 |
| Man-Eating Plant | 49127943 |
| Man-Eating Treasure Chest | 13723605 |
| Manga Ryu-Ran | 38369349 |
| Marine Beast | 29929832 |
| Masaki the Legendary Swordsman | 44287299 |
| Mask of Darkness | 28933734 |
| Masked Sorcerer | 10189126 |
| Master & Expert | 75499502 |
| Mavelus | 59036972 |
| Mechanical Snail | 34442949 |
| Mechanical Spider | 45688586 |
| Mechanicalchaser | 07359741 |
| Meda Bat | 76211194 |
| Mega Thunderball | 21817254 |
| Megamorph | 22046459 |
| Megazowler | 75390004 |
| Meotoko | 53832650 |
| Mesmeric Control | 48642904 |
| Messenger of Peace | 44656491 |
| Metal Detector | 75646520 |
| Metal Dragon | 09293977 |
| Metal Fish | 55998462 |
| Metal Guardian | 68339286 |

| Card | Password |
|------|----------|
| Metalmorph | 68540058 |
| Metalzoa | 50705071 |
| Millennium Golem | 47986555 |
| Millennium Shield | 32012841 |
| Milus Radiant | 07489323 |
| Minar | 32539892 |
| Minomushi Warrior | 46864967 |
| Mirror Force | 44095762 |
| Mirror Wall | 22359980 |
| Misairuzame | 33178416 |
| Molten Destruction | 19384334 |
| Monster Egg | 36121917 |
| Monster Eye | 84133008 |
| Monster Reborn | 83764718 |
| Monster Tamer | 97612389 |
| Monstrous Bird | 35712107 |
| Moon Envoy | 45909477 |
| Mooyan Curry | 58074572 |
| Morinphen | 55784832 |
| Morphing Jar | 33508719 |
| Morphing Jar #2 | 79106360 |
| Mother Grizzly | 57839750 |
| Mountain | 50913601 |
| Mountain Warrior | 04931562 |
| Mr. Volcano | 31477025 |
| Muka Muka | 46657337 |
| Mushroom Man | 14181608 |
| Mushroom Man #2 | 93900406 |
| Musician King | 56907389 |
| M-Warrior #1 | 56342351 |
| M-Warrior #2 | 92731455 |
| Mysterious Puppeteer | 54098121 |
| Mystic Horseman | 68516705 |
| Mystic Lamp | 98049915 |
| Mystic Plasma Zone | 18161786 |
| Mystic Probe | 49251811 |
| Mystic Tomato | 83011277 |
| Mystical Capture Chain | 63515678 |
| Mystical Elf | 15025844 |
| Mystical Moon | 36607978 |
| Mystical Sand | 32751480 |

| Card | Password |
| --- | --- |
| Mystical Sheep #1 | 30451366 |
| Mystical Sheep #2 | 83464209 |
| Mystical Space Typhoon | 05318639 |
| Needle Ball | 94230224 |
| Needle Worm | 81843628 |
| Negate Attack | 14315573 |
| Nekogal #1 | 01761063 |
| Nekogal #2 | 43352213 |
| Nemuriko | 90963488 |
| Neo the Magic Swordsman | 50930991 |
| Nimble Momonga | 22567609 |
| Niwatori | 07805359 |
| Nobleman of Crossout | 71044499 |
| Nobleman of Extermination | 17449108 |
| Numinous Healer | 02130625 |
| Octoberser | 74637266 |
| Ocubeam | 86088138 |
| Ogre of the Black Shadow | 45121025 |
| One-Eyed Shield Dragon | 33064647 |
| Ooguchi | 58861941 |
| Ookazi | 19523799 |
| Orion the Battle King | 02971090 |
| Oscillo Hero | 82065276 |
| Oscillo Hero #2 | 27324313 |
| Painful Choice | 74191942 |
| Pale Beast | 21263083 |
| Panther Warrior | 42035044 |
| Paralyzing Potion | 50152549 |
| Parasite Paracide | 27911549 |
| Parrot Dragon | 62762898 |
| Patrol Robo | 76775123 |
| Peacock | 20624263 |
| Pendulum Machine | 24433920 |
| Penguin Knight | 36039163 |
| Penguin Soldier | 93920745 |
| Petit Angel | 38142739 |
| Petit Dragon | 75356564 |
| Petit Moth | 58192742 |
| Polymerization | 24094653 |
| Pot of Greed | 55144522 |
| Power of Kaishin | 77027445 |

| Card | Password |
| --- | --- |
| Pragtical | 33691040 |
| Premature Burial | 70828912 |
| Prevent Rat | 00549481 |
| Princess of Tsurugi | 51371017 |
| Prisman | 80234301 |
| Prohibition | 43711255 |
| Protector of the Throne | 10071456 |
| Psychic Kappa | 07892180 |
| Pumpking the King of Ghosts | 29155212 |
| Punished Eagle | 74703140 |
| Queen Bird | 73081602 |
| Queen of Autumn Leaves | 04179849 |
| Queen's Double | 05901497 |
| Raigeki | 12580477 |
| Raimei | 56260110 |
| Rainbow Flower | 21347810 |
| Raise Body Heat | 51267887 |
| Rare Fish | 80516007 |
| Ray & Temperature | 85309439 |
| Reaper of the Cards | 33066139 |
| Red Archery Girl | 65570596 |
| Red Medicine | 38199696 |
| Red-Eyes Black Dragon | 74677422 |
| Red-Eyes Black Metal Dragon | 64335804 |
| Reinforcements | 17814387 |
| Relinquished | 64631466 |
| Remove Trap | 51482758 |
| Respect Play | 08951260 |
| Restructer Revolution | 99518961 |
| Reverse Trap | 77622396 |
| Rhaimundos of the Red Sword | 62403074 |
| Right Arm of the Forbidden One | 70903634 |
| Right Leg of the Forbidden One | 08124921 |
| Ring of Magnetism | 20436034 |
| Riryoku | 34016756 |
| Rising Air Current | 45778932 |
| Roaring Ocean Snake | 19066538 |
| Robbin' Goblin | 88279736 |
| Rock Ogre Grotto #1 | 68846917 |
| Rogue Doll | 91939608 |
| Root Water | 39004808 |
| Rose Spectre of Dunn | 32485271 |

| Card | Password |
|------|----------|
| Royal Decree | 51452091 |
| Royal Guard | 39239728 |
| Rude Kaiser | 26378150 |
| Rush Recklessly | 70046172 |
| Ryu-Kishin | 15303296 |
| Ryu-Kishin Powered | 24611934 |
| Ryu-Ran | 02964201 |
| Saber Slasher | 73911410 |
| Saggi the Dark Clown | 66602787 |
| Salamandra | 32268901 |
| Sand Stone | 73051941 |
| Sangan | 26202165 |
| Sea Kamen | 71746462 |
| Sea King Dragon | 23659124 |
| Seal of the Ancients | 97809599 |
| Sebek's Blessing | 22537443 |
| Sectarian of Secrets | 15507080 |
| Senju of the Thousand Hands | 23401839 |
| Seven Tools of the Bandit | 03819470 |
| Shadow Specter | 40575313 |
| Share the Pain | 56830749 |
| Shield & Sword | 52097679 |
| Shining Fairy | 95956346 |
| Shovel Crusher | 71950093 |
| Silver Bow and Arrow | 01557499 |
| Silver Fang | 90357090 |
| Sinister Serpent | 08131171 |
| Skelengel | 60694662 |
| Skelgon | 32355828 |
| Skull Dice | 00126218 |
| Skull Red Bird | 10202894 |
| Skull Servant | 32274490 |
| Skull Stalker | 54844990 |
| Skullbird | 08327462 |
| Sleeping Lion | 40200834 |
| Slot Machine | 03797883 |
| Snake Fang | 00596051 |
| Snakeyashi | 29802344 |
| Snatch Steal | 45986603 |
| Sogen | 86318356 |
| Solemn Judgment | 41420027 |
| Solitude | 84794011 |

| Card | Password |
|------|----------|
| Solomon's Lawbook | 23471572 |
| Sonic Bird | 57617178 |
| Sonic Maid | 38942059 |
| Soul Hunter | 72869010 |
| Soul of the Pure | 47852924 |
| Soul Release | 05758500 |
| Sparks | 76103675 |
| Spear Cretin | 58551308 |
| Spellbinding Circle | 18807108 |
| Spike Seadra | 85326399 |
| Spirit of the Books | 14037717 |
| Spirit of the Harp | 80770678 |
| Stain Storm | 21323861 |
| Star Boy | 08201910 |
| Steel Ogre Grotto #1 | 29172562 |
| Steel Ogre Grotto #2 | 90908427 |
| Steel Scorpion | 13599884 |
| Steel Shell | 02370081 |
| Stim-Pack | 83225447 |
| Stone Armadiller | 63432835 |
| Stone Ogre Grotto | 15023985 |
| Stop Defense | 63102017 |
| Stuffed Animal | 71068263 |
| Succubus Knight | 55291359 |
| Summoned Skull | 70781052 |
| Supporter in the Shadows | 41422426 |
| Swamp Battleguard | 40453765 |
| Sword Arm of Dragon | 13069066 |
| Sword of Dark Destruction | 37120512 |
| Sword of Deep-Seated | 98495314 |
| Sword of Dragon's Soul | 61405855 |
| Swords of Revealing Light | 72302403 |
| Swordsman from a Foreign Land | 85255550 |
| Swordstalker | 50005633 |
| Tailor of the Fickle | 43641473 |
| Tainted Wisdom | 28725004 |
| Takriminos | 44073668 |
| Takuhee | 03170832 |
| Tao the Chanter | 46247516 |
| Temple of Skulls | 00732302 |
| Tenderness | 57935140 |

| Card | Password |
|------|----------|
| Terra the Terrible | 63308047 |
| The 13th Grave | 00032864 |
| The Bewitching Phantom Thief | 24348204 |
| The Bistro Butcher | 71107816 |
| The Cheerful Coffin | 41142615 |
| The Drdek | 08944575 |
| The Eye of Truth | 34694160 |
| The Flute of Summoning Dragon | 43973174 |
| The Forceful Sentry | 42829885 |
| The Furious Sea King | 18710707 |
| The Immortal of Thunder | 84926738 |
| The Inexperienced Spy | 81820689 |
| The Little Swordsman of Aile | 25109950 |
| The Regulation of Tribe | 00296499 |
| The Reliable Guardian | 16430187 |
| The Shallow Grave | 43434803 |
| The Snake Hair | 29491031 |
| The Stern Mystic | 87557188 |
| The Thing That Hides in the Mud | 18180762 |
| The Unhappy Maiden | 51275027 |
| The Wandering Doomed | 93788854 |
| The Wicked Worm Beast | 06285791 |
| Three-Headed Geedo | 78423643 |
| Three-Legged Zombies | 33734439 |
| Thunder Dragon | 31786629 |
| Tiger Axe | 49791927 |
| Time Machine | 80987696 |
| Time Seal | 35316708 |
| Time Wizard | 71625222 |
| Toad Master | 62671448 |
| Togex | 33878931 |
| Toll | 82003859 |
| Tomozaurus | 46457856 |
| Tongyo | 69572024 |
| Toon Alligator | 59383041 |
| Toon Mermaid | 65458948 |
| Toon Summoned Skull | 91842653 |
| Toon World | 15259703 |
| Torike | 80813021 |
| Total Defense Shogun | 75372290 |
| Trakadon | 42348802 |
| Trap Hole | 04206964 |

| Card | Password |
|------|----------|
| Trap Master | 46461247 |
| Trent | 78780140 |
| Trial of Nightmare | 77827521 |
| Tribute to the Doomed | 79759861 |
| Tripwire Beast | 45042329 |
| Turtle Tiger | 37313348 |
| Twin Long Rods #2 | 29692206 |
| Twin-Headed Fire Dragon | 78984772 |
| Twin-Headed Thunder Dragon | 54752875 |
| Two-Headed King Rex | 94119974 |
| Two-Mouth Darkruler | 57305373 |
| Two-Pronged Attack | 83887306 |
| Tyhone | 72842870 |
| Tyhone #2 | 56789759 |
| UFO Turtle | 60806437 |
| Ultimate Offering | 80604091 |
| Umi | 22702055 |
| Umiiruka | 82999629 |
| Unknown Warrior of Fiend | 97360116 |
| Upstart Goblin | 70368879 |
| Uraby | 01784619 |
| Ushi Oni | 48649353 |
| Valkyrion the Magna Warrior | 75347539 |
| Vermillion Sparrow | 35752363 |
| Versago the Destroyer | 50259460 |
| Vile Germs | 39774685 |
| Violent Rain | 94042337 |
| Violet Crystal | 15052462 |
| Vishwar Randi | 78556320 |
| Vorse Raider | 14898066 |
| Waboku | 12607053 |
| Wall of Illusion | 13945283 |
| Warrior Elimination | 90873992 |
| Warrior of Tradition | 56413937 |
| Wasteland | 23424603 |
| Water Element | 03732747 |
| Water Girl | 55014050 |
| Water Magician | 93343894 |
| Water Omotics | 02483611 |
| Waterdragon Fairy | 66836598 |
| Weather Control | 37243151 |

| Card | Password |
| --- | --- |
| Weather Report | 72053645 |
| Whiptail Crow | 91996584 |
| White Hole | 43487744 |
| White Magical Hat | 15150365 |
| Wicked Mirror | 15150371 |
| Widespread Ruin | 77754944 |
| Windstorm of Etaqua | 59744639 |
| Wing Egg Elf | 98582704 |
| Winged Cleaver | 39175982 |
| Winged Dragon, Guardian of the Fortress #1 | 87796900 |
| Wings of Wicked Flame | 92944626 |
| Witch of the Black Forest | 78010363 |
| Witch's Apprentice | 80741828 |
| Witty Phantom | 36304921 |
| Wodan the Resident of the Forest | 42883273 |
| Wood Remains | 17733394 |
| World Suppression | 12253117 |
| Wow Warrior | 69750536 |
| Wretched Ghost of the Attic | 17238333 |
| Yado Karu | 29380133 |
| Yaiba Robo | 10315429 |
| Yamatano Dragon Scroll | 76704943 |
| Yami | 59197169 |
| Yaranzo | 71280811 |
| Zanki | 30090452 |
| Zoa | 24311372 |
| Zombie Warrior | 31339260 |
| Zone Eater | 86100785 |

**BradyGAMES® Publishing**
An Imprint of Pearson Education
800 East 96th Street, Third Floor
Indianapolis, Indiana 46240

**ISBN:** 0-7440-0336-9

**Printing Code:** The rightmost double-digit number is the year of the book's printing; the rightmost single-digit number is the number of the book's printing. For
example, 03-1 shows that the first printing of the book occurred in 2003.

06 05 04 03                                                    4  3  2  1

Manufactured in the United States of America.

# BradyGAMES Staff

| | |
|---|---|
| **Publisher** | David Waybright |
| **Editor-In-Chief** | H. Leigh Davis |
| **Marketing Manager** | Janet Eshenour |
| **Creative Director** | Robin Lasek |
| **Licensing Manager** | Mike Degler |
| **Assistant Marketing Manager** | Susie Nieman |

# Credits

| | |
|---|---|
| **Project Editor** | Christopher Hausermann |
| **Screenshot Editor** | Michael Owen |
| **Book Designers** | Carol Stamile and Doug Wilkins |
| **Production Designer** | Amy Hassos |